# ODD-SHAPED BALLS

Mischief-Makers, Miscreants
and Mad-Hatters of Rugby

# JOHN SCALLY

**MAINSTREAM
PUBLISHING**

EDINBURGH AND LONDON

This book is dedicated to those players who
played for Ireland but were never awarded a cap.

Reprinted 2007

Copyright © John Scally, 2004
All rights reserved
The moral right of the author has been asserted

First published in Great Britain in 2004 by
MAINSTREAM PUBLISHING COMPANY
(EDINBURGH) LTD
7 Albany Street
Edinburgh EH1 3UG

ISBN 9781845960414

This edition, 2005

A catalogue record for this book is available from
the British Library

Typeset in Comic Sans and Janson Text
Printed and bound in Great Britain by
Cox & Wyman Ltd

# Acknowledgements

I am very grateful to the many players, past and present, who shared their personal anecdotes with me. My thanks also to Ollic Campbell, Martina Cleary, Bill McLaren, Brian, Frank and Geraldine O'Driscoll and Tony Ward. Special thanks to Mick Quinn for his amazing treasure trove of stories. I am grateful to Bronagh O'Hanlon for her cartoons. Thanks to Bill Campbell and all at Mainstream for their enthusiastic support of this book.

# Contents

# Introduction

Q: Why do they call it 'rugby'?
A: Because 'assault and battery' was already taken.

Former world boxing champion Chris Eubank tried to stop his
son playing rugby because it is 'the moth vicious thport on
God'th earth'. It is hard to take seriously someone who also
said, 'All the rudiments for success in life are to be found in
ironing trousers.' Eubank's comment shows that he
fundamentally misunderstands the sport and criminally fails to
appreciate its innate aesthetic appeal. At its best, rugby really is
'the beautiful game'.

I should have been a great rugby player. I had the height.
The only thing I lacked was even a tiny amount of skill. As my
rugby career floundered, my kind cousin decided to open up

another sporting career for me. He always claimed that I had 'a good eye' and on that basis decided I would be good at shooting. As he was an accomplished marksman, I trusted him implicitly. A Sunday afternoon was chosen for my investiture in my uncle's farmyard in the west of Ireland. An empty Batchelors peas tin was put up on the wall and I was instructed on how to take aim. I squeezed the trigger and nearly fell over with the kick from the rifle. I looked up, but the Batchelors peas tin was still gloriously intact. I could tell from the horror on my cousin's face that something terrible had happened. At first I couldn't find the problem, but after a minute or two my eyes turned to the clothes-line, about 20 yards away from the wall. There was now a big, gaping hole in my uncle's best shirt. Little wonder that my uncle has been shirty with me since.

Having failed dismally as a player, I had to content myself with being a fan. This book is the fruit of a lifelong addiction. Rugby talk is invariably fascinating for many reasons, not least of which is its delightful brand of articulate bitchery and polite savagery. The comments represent, in condensed form, the spontaneous venom of some of the thwarted high achievers: charming little darts, wicked little stabs, though sometimes not so little, which are merciless, battering some poor unfortunate without relief or hesitation. The following collection captures the sorrow, pain, elation, despair, affection, hostility and above all humour which are the fruits of this consuming passion.

If laughter be the food of rugby, play on. If you didn't have humour, you couldn't have rugby, given the often fluctuating fortunes of every team in the world. 'You can't always get what you want', so sang the Rolling Stones. There are more defeats than victories on the big day. Rugby is one of the few entertainments where, no matter how many times you go back, you never know the ending. This collection compiles the highs and lows of the players inside sweaty, smelly dressing-rooms, of the managers and fans without whom rugby would cease to exist.

# Introduction

It's really about beating your enemy which, wherever the game is played, is invariably England. This book also serves a serious purpose. It proves beyond reasonable doubt the sociological truth that the relationship between the English and the rest of the rugby world is based on trust and understanding: they don't trust us and we don't understand them!

It may be that Irish personalities feature somewhat disproportionately in this book. If so, I make no apologies for the fact. It has nothing to do with nationalist sentiment. In the history of international rugby, Ireland has won very few titles. On the World Cup and Grand Slam index, Ireland does not feature very prominently. Yet no student of the game would disagree that Ireland has given international rugby more than its fair share of great characters. In this category are people like Jack MacCaulay. He was said to be the first married man to be capped in international rugby in 1887 – according to rugby folklore he got wed just to get leave of absence from work to play for Ireland! Even club players have entered rugby's international informal hall of fame with their celebrated wit. A case in point is Sam Hutton of Malone, not least because of his famous chat-up line, 'Excuse me, darling, haven't you met me somewhere before?' They may not know how to win many titles but they certainly know how to have a laugh. If there is a doubting Thomas who would challenge this claim, then *Odd-Shaped Balls* is literally the book of evidence.

In theory, the rugby fields are a theatre in which an attempt is made to establish superior skill. In practice, they are often a forum where an engaging battle of wits occurs, with the figures on the scoreboard being momentarily the last thing on anyone's mind. Sometimes the results are bemusing. More often, as we shall see, they are amusing. This collection reveals the unquenchable, insatiable wit that smoulders unseen under the mute, impassive faces of the world's toughest men. The result is a wry, idiosyncratic and sometimes bizarre catalogue of comic creations. The veracity of many of the stories told in this collection would not stand up to rigorous scrutiny. They are not meant to be statements of fact but intended to give a laugh or at least bring a smile.

It is said that humour and good taste are mutually exclusive. That is probably particularly the case with rugby humour. This is not the book for those who love political correctness.

# ONE

## England's Ruck and Rollers

### Heaven sent

Will Carling faced God at the throne of Heaven with Gareth Edwards and Phil Bennett. God said to them, 'Before granting you a place at my side, I must ask for your beliefs.'

Bennett stared God directly in the eye and said, 'I believe rugby is the meaning of life. Nothing else has brought so much joy to so many. I have devoted my life to spreading the gospel of rugby.'

God was moved by his passion and eloquence and said, 'You are a man of true faith. Sit by me at my right hand.'

He then turned to Wales's most famous rugby son. 'Now, my child, tell me what you believe in.'

Gareth answered, 'I believe courage, bravery, loyalty, teamwork, dedication and commitment are the soul of life and I dedicated my career to living up to those ideals.'

God replied, 'You have spoken well, my child. Sit by me at my left hand.'

Then he turned to Carling. 'And you, Mr Carling, what is it that you believe?'

Carling gave him a withering look and replied, 'I believe that you are sitting in my chair.'

## The future king and I

In the mid-1990s, there was much media speculation about a doomed romance between Princess Diana and England's rugby captain Will Carling. Carling strongly denied the rumours. After news of the alleged affair had been leaked to the press, Prince Charles had to present the International Championship trophy to Carling in a match in which the captain failed to get a try. The prince said, 'I'm sorry you didn't score.'

Carling replied, 'At last. Somebody believes me.'

## Probably the best

Carling has a more sociable side. On the Lions tour in 1993, Carling was rechristened 'O'Carling' when he started drinking Guinness.

After captaining Ireland to a defeat against England, Willie Anderson was talking to Will Carling at the dinner in the Hilton. There was a very serious atmosphere so he asked Carling to go downstairs with him for a 'wee drink'. Willie asked him what he wanted and Carling said a gin and tonic so he ordered two. He nearly dropped dead when the barman charged him £10. When he asked him could he charge it to his room the barman said no. Then Willie pulled out two £5 notes from the Bank of Northern Ireland but the barman immediately said he couldn't take these. Willie said to Carling he would have to pay for the drinks. When Carling pulled out his wallet, Anderson claims there was a combination to it; Carling was not renowned as a big spender. Although Ireland lost the match, at least Willie had the satisfaction of making the English captain buy him a drink, which was said to be a more difficult task than beating England!

## It says in the papers

During his time as England captain Carling was constantly featured in the media. Some of the coverage was flattering, much of it not. As an illustration of the distortions in the print media, a rugby fan told the 'parable' of a man from Pakistan who fell under a Tube train in London and was killed. *The Times* reported it straight, *The Sun* that an asylum seeker had disrupted British Rail schedules, *The Scotsman* that a Scot had been killed at Heathrow, the *Irish Press* that British Rail had murdered an innocent Irishman, and the *Daily Mail* that Will Carling had his travel schedule disrupted because of a mishap on British Rail.

## A misunderstood man

Carling was not universally loved by his teammates. On one occasion when his club side Harlequins played Wasps, it was a typically robust match. After a heated ruck, where boots were flying with more frequency than planes at an airport, everyone picked themselves off the muddy pitch to reveal the man at the bottom of the pile of bodies. It was Carling. He had a huge gash under his eye. The referee, slightly shocked that the English captain should be the victim of such thuggery, asked, 'Right, own up, who did this?'

Immediately, Carling's teammate, Richard Langhorn, piped up, 'Take your pick, ref, it could have been any one of twenty-nine of us.'

In 1989, Carling was expected to lead England to the Grand Slam, but Wales tripped them up at the last hurdle. The English team were scheduled to meet England's most famous royal at the time. The equerry of the Princess of Wales came into the English dressing-room and said to Carling, 'She'll ask you what your team have said about losing the game and the Grand Slam.'

Carling asked, 'When I'm telling her, do I have to leave out all the cursing and swearing?'

'Certainly.'

'In that case they haven't mentioned it at all.'

Before Austin Healey, Carling was the England player with an exceptional capacity to rub people up the wrong way. Carling went up to Leicester to play for Harlequins in a league match, in a fixture that was being filmed by *Rugby Special*. After the match, Carling was set upon by a Leicester supporter who punched him on the chin. It was widely reported afterwards that it was the first time the fan had hit the sh*t.

Carling has written a number of books but is unlikely to be writing a book on how to win friends and influence people. Over the years, Carling was at the forefront of the debate over the vexed question of whether, and to what extent, rugby should turn professional, with all the ferocious protestations and the growing bitterness between administrators and players. This antagonism was graphically revealed in Carling's description of the RFU Committee as '57 old farts', which caused him to be stripped of the captaincy of the English team.

## Men only

Cricket is often considered to be a bastion of male chauvinist pigs. Hence the notice displayed at many cricket clubs: 'No Dogs or Women'. For over 200 years the MCC, Marylebone Cricket Club, adhered to a No Women policy. This meant no women members, no women in the pavilion on match days and no women guests allowed. In 1988, a poll was taken on the revolutionary suggestion of allowing women into the pavilion as guests. Not surprisingly, the motion was overwhelmingly defeated. Three years later, another motion was put to members. This time the question was: should women be allowed to join the 20-year waiting list? Again, this innovative proposal was roundly rejected. Many people might have misgivings about these chauvinistic tendencies. The MCC, though, rejoice in them. The move to give women a greater role in cricket came at the time when Will Carling had got into serious trouble for making the '57 old farts' comment. Sir Oliver Popplewell, MCC president, responded immediately, 'Well, you won't find 57 old farts here. There are 18,000 of us.'

## Dawson's pique

Another English international who had problems with officialdom is Matt Dawson. After having a successful tour with the Lions in South Africa in 1997, Dawson went on the Lions tour to Australia in 2001 with high hopes. His great expectations were quickly shattered. His newspaper column spoke of his disenchantment with the team's preparation and criticised the team management. It appeared on the morning of the First Test and initially it seemed he would be sent home. The threat of banishment hung in the air for a period. Things came to a climax when a crisis meeting was called between players and management. The Lions were captained by Martin Johnson, who lived by the creed: minimum words, maximum impact. His brief intervention at the meeting was the decisive one. He simply said that if Dawson was sent home, he would be on the next plane. Issue closed.

Ironically, Dawson got away scot-free from what in the era of Bill Beaumont would be considered a sacking offence for an England rugby international: he shaved his legs, donned a wig and dressed up as woman! What was worse, he even did it on national television. The reason for his brief flirtation with cross-dressing was not, as Dan Luger suggested, that he was an apprentice transvestite, but that he was appearing as a mystery guest on the popular BBC series *A Question of Sport*, where top sportspeople who are up for a laugh routinely embarrass themselves. After his appearance on the programme, his fellow internationals Paul Grayson, Mike Tindall and Ben Cohen claimed that Dawson was the ugliest woman ever to appear on television and threatened not to pay their TV licences in the future in protest.

Following England's World Cup victory in 2003, Dawson was one of the English players to cash in by publishing his autobiography, *Nine Lives*. His teammate Mike Catt was reported to be furious because Dawson had 'stolen' the obvious title for his book!

## Backhander

One of Dawson's teammates who also got into hot water was Neil Back. 'The hand of God and the hand of Diego' is one of the most famous incidents of ethical dimensions in world sport. The explanation given by Diego Maradona of Argentina after he deflected the ball with his hand over the advancing England goalkeeper Peter Shilton in the 1986 World Cup was that the ball was helped into the net by 'the hand of God'. His goal helped Argentina to victory and they went on to take the World Cup.

The most talked about 'ethical incident' in rugby occurred in the final moments of the Heineken Cup final in 2002. Munster were trailing Leicester and were driving hard for their opponents' line when they were awarded a set scrum some five metres out from goal. It was crucial to win this ball and set up a final drive for possible victory. As the Munster scrum-half was about to put the ball into the scrum, Neil Back's infamous 'hand of God' backhander knocked the ball from Peter Stringer's grasp into the Leicester scrum and the ball was lost to Leicester. The referee had taken up a position opposite the incoming ball and did not see the incident. The controversy spawned a new joke:

Q: What's the difference between Tim Henman and Neil Back?

A: Neil Back is much better with his backhand.

## England's Ruck and Rollers

### Injury time

A chronic injury sustained with Leicester meant that Austin Healey was forced to miss the 2003 World Cup. One of his English teammates was not as sympathetic as might be expected and said, 'Austin's been injured so long we've changed his name to "I can't believe he's not better".'

Healey is nothing if not original. In 1999, he was brought before a hearing for stamping on London Irish scrum-half Kevin Putt's head. Healey's defence was novel: 'It was the only place I could put my foot.'

### Woodward's wonderful world

England's focus and obsessive will to win the 2003 World Cup can be largely traced back to their then coach Clive Woodward. As a player, Woodward won 21 England caps, culminating in the 1980 Grand Slam. A stylish outside-centre, with wonderful hands, he also toured twice with the Lions. It was as a coach, though, that he really excelled.

One of Woodward's favourite phrases is 'massively full-on'. This phrase took on a new connotation during the World Cup tournament. Asked how he reacted to being kept awake by chants of 'Boring! Boring!' from Australian fans, he replied, 'I was with my wife in bed at the time – fortunately, I realised what they were actually referring to.'

Woodward was magnanimous in victory after the World Cup final win. He did have some reservations about the South African referee Andre Watson's performance in the final, which saw a number of contentious penalties going to Australia. Hence Nick Hancock's comment, 'The World Cup final produced Australia's sports personality of the year – the referee!'

England's victory in the competition came as no surprise in Uruguay. Before playing England in the World Cup, Uruguay's coach Diego Ormaechea was asked to explain his side's preparation for their clash with Woodward's warriors. He replied, 'We have an English trainer with us and we asked him what we should do to prepare and he said, "Just play golf."'

Surprisingly, not everyone in England was eulogising Woodward's team. A rugby league fan wrote to the *Daily Telegraph* and said, 'If rugby union is the game they play in heaven, then, God, please send me to hell.'

After France's impressive defeat of Ireland and England's unimpressive performance against Wales in the quarter-finals, many pundits predicted that the French would sweep to victory over England in the semi-final. Not so Ireland's leading rugby commentator, Michael Corcoran. He confidently predicted that 'England will upset the apple tart'. Another of Michael's gems came the day Ireland claimed the 2004 Triple Crown with a win over Scotland: 'Ronan O'Gara has his boots on the right foot.'

### Go, Jonny, go

In the run-up to the 2003 World Cup, the golden boys of English rugby and English football, Jonny Wilkinson MBE and David Beckham OBE, featured in a TV campaign for a sporting company that received a lot of airplay. Wilkinson was featured teaching Becks to strike a rugby ball. On the eve of England's opening match in the Rugby World Cup, England faced Turkey to decide who would compete in the European football championships in 2004. England's best chance in the second leg of the game came when they were awarded a penalty. Beckham stepped up to take it but blazed the ball high over the bar. Afterwards, Wilkinson joked, 'David's been spending too much time with me!'

Wilkinson's last-gasp drop-goal against Australia in the World Cup final guaranteed him sporting immortality. Watching the score on a television replay one could not but be reminded of David Acfield's immortal commentary: 'Strangely, in slow-motion replay the ball seemed to hang in the air for even longer.'

After the win, Wilkinson's popularity went through not just the roof but the stratosphere. This was most evident when he appeared as a guest on the popular *Parkinson* programme. When he walked on the set, he got a rapturous standing ovation, prompting Michael Parkinson to observe, 'I've been doing this programme for 3,000 years and that's the first time I've ever seen a standing ovation for a guest.'

Jonny has poked gentle fun at the Welsh tendency to recruit 'nationals' from down under to play for 'their country' under the grandparentage rule. He tells the following story for illustrative purposes.

Wales have a serious shortage of world-class defenders. Apparently, in 2001, the then coach, Graham Henry was so stuck for a quality back to play against England one day that he decided to play a goose. Happily, the goose had Welsh grandparents. To everyone's surprise, the goose had a brilliant first half. One minute it was back in the defence making great tackles, the next it was up in the attack kicking points from every angle. At half-time, Henry was delighted, as Wales had a huge lead. As everyone ran back onto the pitch for the second half, the ref started chatting to the goose and said, 'Great first half you played there, my friend, you must be really fit.'

'Thanks,' replied the goose, 'I try to keep myself fit but it's difficult finding the time, so I try to do an hour or two in the gym each morning before work.'

'What do you do, then?' asked the ref.

'I'm a lawyer,' replied the goose. Immediately, the ref brandished a red card and sent the goose off. The furious Welsh team gathered around the ref and started complaining. 'I had no other option. It was as clear as day. Professional fowl.' After his heroics in helping England to the World Cup, Wilkinson was given the freedom of Newcastle, and it was suggested that he should be employed to promote the city. The suggestion was that because of his apparently divine powers he should be filmed walking on the River Tyne.

## Fowl language

Wilkinson has brought a whole new audience to rugby, including more women and gay men. Hence he was described during the World Cup as 'the hottest thing down under since Shane Warne's urine sample'. Among these new fans is one of Britain's best-known television personalities, Graham Norton. Admittedly, he admires Jonny more for his bum than for his rugby genius. This became apparent when Wilkinson was involved in a car accident shortly after the English team's triumphant celebration of the World Cup win. Details of the accident were shrouded in mystery. Norton, though, had no problems going public about it: 'My theory is that he was rear-ended. It's more of a recurring fantasy, really!'

### Captain Fantastic?

Wilkinson kicked all of England's 24 points in the 17-point defeat of France in the 2003 World Cup semi-final. In the match, England's captain, the self-titled 'Terminator in shorts', Martin Johnson, had given away a few easy penalties which France had fortunately missed. A few days before the World Cup final against Australia, some of the key English players were at one of their final press conferences when Lawrence Dallaglio was asked: 'What does Martin Johnson bring to the team?'

Displaying what Sir Clive Woodward calls 'T-Cup', i.e. 'Thinking correctly under pressure', quick as a flash Dallaglio replied, 'Well, there's the concession of a few needless penalties for a start!'

Mind you, the French fans were even more scathing about their team's capitulation to England in the second half. The national daily sports paper *L'Équipe* responded to France's rain-soaked exit from the tournament at the hands of the English by saying, 'Les Bleus: Soluble in Water'.

After leading England to the World Cup, Johnson triumphantly led his team to Buckingham Palace, where the team had its picture taken with the Queen. Afterwards, Johnson said, 'It will be a unique picture with that dog in it.' A spokesman confirmed later that he was referring to a corgi that had run into shot and not Her Majesty.

England's World Cup victory has brought them a whole new profile. This may be a good thing, considering what happened the last time they visited Canada a few years previously. When they attended a reception, one of their hosts enquired, 'It's great to have you soccer-ball guys here. Which one of you is Beck-Ham?'

A prophet is not appreciated in his homeland. English winger Jason Robinson expected to make a glorious return from the World Cup. He was in for a let-down: 'When I got back home, the heating was off, the house was freezing and there was mouldy food in the fridge. I'll have to remind my wife about that.'

## So long

At the end of the Six Nations Championship in 2004, another World Cup winner, Jason Leonard, announced his retirement from international rugby. Given his exalted status in world rugby he might have expected his international colleagues to be full of nostalgia. But Austin Healey's reaction to the news was typically edgy: 'I'm sure the lads will be glad to see him gone. There will be more food for everyone else now! He's been their icon of rugby throughout the ages – the stone age, the ice age and the iron age!'

## Sleeping beauty

Following a series of sterling performances on the English wing, John Bentley was chosen to tour with the Lions in 1997. One of the key players on that tour was the bald wonder Keith Wood. However, Woodie's one blemish was also to emerge on the trip. Bentley had the misfortune to be rooming with him. As a result of his shoulder problems, Keith could only sleep in one position. He propped two pillows under both shoulders and as soon as he began to sleep he started snoring loudly. After seven sleepless nights, Bentley could take no more and sought medical advice. On the eighth night, as soon as Woodie started sleeping, Bentley kissed him on the cheek. For the next three nights Woodie lay awake in case Bentley made further advances on him.

## Jonah doesn't live in whale

In 1997, England played a 26–26 draw with the All Blacks at Twickenham. David Rees scored a try for England and gave a good performance on the wing – even though he faced the apparently impossible task of marking the mighty Jonah Lomu. Before the game, Rees had an unusual tactical talk with Clive Woodward. Woodward asked, 'Right, Reesy, how are we going to deal with this guy Jonah Lomu?'

'OK, Clive, I'm gonna angle my run so I push him towards the touchline and use it as an extra man, just forcing him out for a lineout.'

'OK. But what happens if he cuts inside you?'

'Well, I'll angle it so that he's running back towards our cover defence and Kyran Bracken will be there to help smother him and bring him down.'

'Great. But what happens if he runs straight at you?'

'OK, if he runs straight at me I'll get some crap from the ground and throw it in his face, blinding him.'

'What? But there won't be any crap on the ground.'

'When he's running straight at me, Clive, yes there will!'

## The road not taken

Lawrence Dallaglio's mother has strong Irish roots. Accordingly, Lawrence could have played for Ireland. In 1994, the combined talents of Dean Richards, Ben Clarke, Tim Rodber, Steve Ojomoh and Neil Back were keeping Dallaglio out of the senior team, although he had played for England at a number of levels. His ancestry became known to the Irish selectors and they made an approach. Typically, the advance was an unconventional one. Dallaglio was at home when he received a call. 'Lawrence, Noel Murphy here. We heard you like a few pints of the black stuff and were wondering if you'd like to wear the green shirt of Ireland.'

## Time to say goodbye?

A few years later, when Dallaglio was appointed captain of England for the first time, he met his predecessor, Phil de Glanville. Phil wished Lawrence the best of luck and ushered him aside, saying, 'Just a little advice, as tradition goes, from one outgoing England captain to the next. Take these.'

He handed Lawrence three envelopes.

'If you fail to lead England to victory,' he said, 'open an envelope, and inside you will find some invaluable advice as to how to proceed.'

Immediately after Lawrence's first match, a 15–15 draw against Australia at Twickenham, he remembered Phil's envelopes and opened the first one. 'Blame the referee,' it said.

He walked confidently into the press conference and said, 'Well, there wasn't much between the teams, really. In a match like that, small mistakes can change the complexion of the game completely and in that respect I felt that the ref made some decisions that went against us, which had a big bearing on the final outcome.'

The journalists nodded wisely. Phil's advice was working well.

Another defeat against the All Blacks quickly followed. Bad news – Dallaglio would have to use the second of the three envelopes.

'Blame the place-kicker,' it said. Off the aspiring Captain Fantastic went to face the media.

'Well, I thought it was nip and tuck, we had them under pressure, but unfortunately Mike Catt didn't have the best of days with the old shooting boots and so the chances slipped away.'

Again the journalists seemed satisfied with his response. Thank God for these get-out-of-jail-free envelopes, Dallaglio reflected, though he had still failed to take England to victory and knew he was storing up trouble for himself.

His third game was against the All Blacks at Twickenham. Serious pressure. England began brightly and appeared to be in the ascendancy, but the All Blacks started to haul back. The match ended in a draw. Dallaglio was gutted not to have won. There was only one consolation: help was at hand. He walked into the dressing-room, looking forward to some first-class advice from the third and last white envelope. He rummaged in his bag, pulled it out and tore it open. The advice was simple: 'Start writing out three new envelopes.'

## Hookers and swingers

Phil de Glanville was playing golf one day when he walked past his teammate Nigel Redman desperately trying to hack a ball out of the bunker. He stopped and asked, 'Nigel, why are you trying to use a four iron to hit the ball out of the bunker?'

Nigel replied, 'It wasn't a bloody bunker when I started.'

Phil tried to console him: 'That's maybe why it is said that golf and masturbation have at least one thing in common. Both are a lot more satisfying to do than they are to watch.'

## Looking after number one

In the heady days of amateurism, a coach was a four-wheeled vehicle to get you to the stadium. In the Clive Woodward era, the coach is cast in a different mould. Woodward is a big admirer of the Royal Marines and the England team often found themselves down at Lympstone in South Devon to be bonded into a unit as tight and fearsome as the Marines themselves.

On one such expedition, the squad went orienteering on Bodmin Moor. The England players were fully briefed by their Marine instructors before being dispatched in pairs, with instructions on where to camp overnight and where to report the following morning. Jason Leonard was paired with Jeremy Guscott. With great difficulty, the pair had reached the first few checkpoints and the spot where they were due to spend the night. After sharing out the hardtack, they settled into their tent, only to be disturbed by a low growling noise coming from somewhere nearby. Guscott blurted out, 'What's going on?'

The deadly duo could soon make out a massive four-legged shape just outside the tent. Leonard said, 'Oh hell! I think it's what the Marines warned us about – it's the Beast of Bodmin.'

Guscott started to struggle into his clothes, much to Leonard's annoyance. 'Keep quiet. Remember, the Marines said our only chance was to keep absolutely quiet, and hope he goes away!' Guscott paid no attention, continued dressing and lifted up the back flap of the tent.

'What on earth are you doing?' whispered Leonard. 'You know what the Marines said.'

'I'm going to run for it,' Guscott coolly replied.

'Are you mad? Don't you remember what they said . . . no one can outrun the beast of Bodmin.'

'I know that, but I can sure as hell outrun you, you great lardass.'

## Stan the man

During the 1991 World Cup campaign, Clive Woodward was recruited by ITV to give expert comment. The most memorable moment of his commentary came in the Australia–Western Samoa game. When the camera homed in on the Samoan hooker, Woodward remarked in a very earnest fashion, 'That's the hooker. They call him Stan . . . that's his name.'

An analyst's job is to mix insight with comedy. Much of the time, though, the comedy is unintentional, as when Sky pundit Andy Gray remarked, 'Any footballer who takes drugs should be hammered.' Asked to predict the eventual winners, Woodward said: 'The Aussies don't look in the same league as the All Blacks. They were busy without doing anything. A bit like election agents.'

As a filler before a Japan match, ITV did a short interview with Woodward's former Lions teammate Tony Ward about Ireland's progress in the tournament. Ward is not on the big side, so when Woodward was asked for his take on things he joked, 'Ah, Wardie, there is a rumour going around that you'll be lining out for the Japanese today. You're the right height, apparently.'

Clive Woodward has never lacked confidence. Kevin Keegan famously said, 'Argentina are the second-best side in the world – and there's no higher praise than that.' Woodward thought otherwise and was rewarded when he led England to the World Cup.

After he became English coach, he was asked how he would cope with disagreements with senior players. It is joked that Woodward replied, 'I will handle things the Brian Clough way. Whenever a player has a problem we will talk about it for 20 minutes and I will listen carefully to what he has to say. Then we'll agree that I was right.'

Woodward is no fan of David Campese and was not amused when the BBC decided to get Campo to present the English rugby team with their award for Team of the Year on their

## England's Ruck and Rollers

*Sports Personality of the Year* awards show in 2003, after Campo's withering comments about the English team before the World Cup. In the wake of England's victory in the tournament, Campo famously walked down London's Oxford Street wearing a St George's Cross sandwich board that read: 'I Admit the Best Team Won'. Campo does not share Hugh Grant's opinion of Britain in the smash-hit film *Love Actually* as 'a small but proud nation of Shakespeare, the Beatles, David Beckham's right foot – and indeed of David Beckham's left foot'. His animosity to England was evident before Australia played 'the Poms' in the 1991 World Cup final, when Campese was asked whether he would play for England. Campo replied, 'I wouldn't play for England if you paid me.'

It cannot be confirmed that Woodward objected to Campo being described as 'the great Australian winger' and referred to him instead as a 'great whinger'. Neither has it been proven that Sir Clive is the source of one the more recent riddles about Campo.

Q: Why do all the bulbs in David Campese's home only have eight watts?

A: Because he refuses to have anything in his house that is brighter than he is.

Sir Clive was very gracious, though, when England ended its long unbeaten home run against Ireland in 2004. The defeat immediately spawned a rash of jokes. One notice appeared:

> For Sale: one chariot (low-swinging, sweet type), in urgent need of repair (wheels have come off again). One careless owner, details from Clive. Tel: Twickenham 19–13.

Another came in the form of a death notice:

> In Memoriam Slam, G: passed away 6 March 2004, sorely missed by Clive and the boys.

## Odd-Shaped Balls

### All or nothing

With 71 caps and 396 points for England, Rob Andrew had a glittering career. He missed out, though, on a career as a philosopher. He once said, 'There is no such thing as "a lack of confidence". You either have it or you don't.'

### French lessons

British and Irish teams sometimes have linguistic problems when they travel to France. The former Irish manager Pat Whelan had great problems when Ireland played France with his pronunciation of Émile Ntamack. His description was 'those guys have a guy called Nattermack'.

In 1994, Dewi Morris was recalled to the English team for the French match in Parc des Princes. Dewi had been involved in a huge selection battle between him and Kyran Bracken. After Ireland had beaten England at Twickenham two weeks previously, Bracken's was one of the heads to roll. Dewi was determined to make his mark and make the scrum-half position his own. He was completely psyched up. France, though, had lost their six previous encounters with England and were out for revenge. It was a ferociously physical contest. The French were repeatedly robbing the English of try-scoring opportunities by killing the ball. Eventually, Dewi snapped and raced up to the referee, screaming in his less than perfect French: 'Monsieur, monsieur, le ballon, le ballon, le Français non releasee, s'il vous plaît, Monsieur?'

The referee Stephen Hilditch turned to him and said in his lovely Irish lilt,

'That's OK, Dewi. By the way, this might surprise you but I can actually understand English.'

### Yes, Prime Minister

After England's Grand Slam victory against France at Twickenham in 1991, amid the post-match changing-room disarray and celebrations, Mick 'the Munch' Skinner decided to take an early bath so that he could get on the beer undisturbed. The then Prime Minister John Major, an enthusiastic rugby fan, was escorted into the dressing-room by the president of the RFU to congratulate the winning team. The first person they met was a naked Mick Skinner with a towel in his left hand and his privates in his right hand. The Munch held out his right hand and, in his best Geordie accent and his typical vernacular, said, 'Yo, John. Top man, large, bosh, put it there, how's it hanging?'

Despite knowing where Skinner's right hand had just been, the PM shook it without any apparent qualms and retorted, 'Obviously not as well as you, Mr Skinner.'

A variation of the story has Skinner greeting HRH Prince William in the home dressing-room before an England international at Twickenham. Prince William offered his hand for a handshake and Skinner shook it and said, 'Afternoon, sir. How's it hanging?'

After the next home match, Prince William was again brought into the England dressing-room to congratulate the victorious team. When he was reintroduced to Skinner, he said: 'Well done, Mr Skinner. And before you ask, may I inform you it's hanging very well.'

## In the Bath

In the early 1990s, the spa town of Bath was home to the kings of rugby, largely because of Jack Rowell, who transformed them from a team of virtual no-hopers into the cream of the crop. The area around Gloucester, Bath and Bristol is the hub of a hotbed of English rugby. Bath's status in English rugby during the 1990s is comparable to that of the Liverpool FC team of the '70s and '80s or Manchester United in the '90s.

Rowell's Bath was not a club for the hypersensitive. Jon Callard was nicknamed 'Zanussi' because, his colleagues claimed, his head was the shape of a microwave.

Rowell is a great believer in the power of positive thinking.

He famously said, 'There's only one man allowed to say "there's nothing wrong with defeat" and that's Nelson Mandela's chiropodist.'

The Bath players took that message to heart. Hence former England international Ben Clarke's comment, 'At Bath, we won many a game in the last minute. We had so many great escapes, I half-expected to look across to the replacement bench and see Steve McQueen.'

Jack Rowell was once asked what it was like to be a top rugby coach. He replied, 'You have fifteen players in a team. Seven hate your guts and the other eight are making up their minds.'

## The Old Vic

However, Rowell was ahead of his time in the old days of amateurism and created a very commercially advanced environment. One incident illustrates this and provides an interesting metaphor for the changing face of rugby. Steve Ojomoh picked up a nasty injury in training. Bath's team secretary informed his teammates that Ojomoh had received a detached retina. This prompted his international colleague Victor Ubogu to say, 'I'm not happy about that. I've been here much longer than him and I'm still living in a club flat.'

Victor did not appreciate everything Rowell did for him. Rowell's rigorous pre-season physical regime left him sore all over. With every bone in his body aching, and discovering he had pain in places he didn't even know existed, Ubogu was asked to comment on Rowell's contribution to his career. Victor replied, 'Everything I have I owe to him and some day I'll get him back.'

In an attempt to increase bonding and to break the monotony, the Bath management organised for the squad to do some training with the Commandos. Their assignment was to run around the Citadel twice, in teams of six , carrying a heavy log. Four men carrying, two resting but running alongside, all in rotation. On Victor Ubogu's team, Victor was nominated to start in the relief two, not actually carrying the log. As his team charged out of the gates they left most of the teams behind. The only problem was that they left Victor behind too! On their second lap, they were a team of five, not six, because there was still no sign of Victor. Twenty minutes after they got to the finishing line, Victor came puffing in. He was asked, 'Victor, how's the team bonding going?'

'If I don't know these f\*\*kers after ten years, this f\*\*king won't help!'

Before England went to the 1995 World Cup in South Africa, they were warned about the thin air they would face when playing on the high veld of Pretoria, and how hard it would be to breathe. When they arrived in Durban, they went out for their first training session on a pitch by the beach. Halfway through the session and only half a mile from the sea, Victor Ubogu was blowing hard at the pace of the session and, as he got back, was heard to say, 'Christ, this altitude is killing me.'

## Passion denied

While Jack Rowell was happy to see his players profiting from the game, he did not allow commercial activities to distract them from their main focus: playing winning rugby. He did not agree with Dick Greenwood's assertion that 'The amateur rugby union player has an inalienable right to play like a pillock.' Bath's work ethic under Rowell was second to none. One story which typifies the pressure Rowell put on his players concerns Jim Waterman. His son was doing his biology homework and asked his seemingly perpetually exhausted father if he knew what a condom was. Waterman's answer was, 'Of course I do, I've bloody well been carrying one around in my wallet for months!'

# Odd-Shaped Balls

## Not simple Simon

Simon Geoghegan lit up Bath rugby in the early 1990s. His performance was not always enhanced by his teammates. He was rooming with a player who shall remain nameless the night before a big game in November 1995. His colleague got thirsty during the night and disposed of a glass of water in the bathroom. The next morning when Geoghegan went to retrieve his contact lenses he discovered that his 'friend' had unwittingly drunk them along with the glass of water.

## Searching for love

One rugby player who attracted more than his share of female attention was Bath's Jeremy Guscott. After his final performance in an England shirt in the 101–10 points win over Tonga in the 1999 World Cup, when he scored a trademark spectacular solo try, running the length of the pitch, Jeremy was a guest speaker at a charity function. He spoke amusingly on rugby. After he had finished, the organiser said to the audience, 'I hope you'll have some questions for our distinguished visitor. I mean, what does one ask someone so accomplished and famous?' A female voice piped up from the back row, 'Is he married?'

## Like a bridge under troubled waters

Bath were due to play Llanelli in the Heineken European Cup quarter-final. The match had already been postponed once due to heavy rain. For three days the rain had fallen incessantly, like a biblical plague. The Bath players were asked to leave the hotel and walk to the ground, which was ten minutes away. The rain was lashing down. Halfway to the ground, Mark 'Ronnie' Regan stopped and shouted to the rest of the team, 'Great news, guys, it's stopped raining.' It hadn't stopped raining. He was just walking under a bridge.

## Guess when we're coming to dinner?

Jon Hall was a great back-row forward for Bath. While he was captain of the club he liked to think it gave him a certain cachet. After a victory in a Courage League game, the Bath players decided they wanted to go for a meal in the hottest new restaurant in the area. The problem was that everybody else wanted to eat there, so they couldn't get a booking until 10.30 that night. When Hall heard this, he was not happy; he claimed it was too late and convinced his teammates that he could get an earlier booking using his position on the team. All the players crowded around the telephone to observe his negotiating skills. 'Hello, my friend booked a table with you earlier for 10.30 tonight and I know it's a very busy Saturday night for you but I was wondering if there was any possibility that you could fit us in earlier . . . My name is Jon Hall . . . yes, that Jon Hall, the captain of the Bath rugby team . . . Oh no, I couldn't possibly allow you to go to a lot of trouble just for me . . . Well, the last thing I would want you to think is that because of my status in rugby I'm expecting any special treatment . . . Well, if you absolutely insist it's no trouble to you, that would be fantastic . . . fine, fine that's so good of you, I can't thank you enough. You've made all of us very happy. See you soon.'

His Bath colleagues were awestruck with his apparent influence. Their admiration was quickly dissipated, though, when they asked him what time they would now be eating.

Hall announced with a flourish: '10.15!'

## A shepherd's . . .

At one stage Bath played Leinster in a friendly and won easily. Hall gave a man-of-the-match performance. Two of the Bath officials went over to console the Leinster management. They said all the right things, like how unlucky Leinster were, and asked what the Leinster contingent thought of the Bath players. The Leinster duo expressed their great admiration for

Hall. One of the Bath officials said, 'He's a shepherd, you know.'

Quick as a flash, Leinster selector Ned Thornton replied, 'And he's in the British Army.'

There followed a pantomime-like scene. 'Oh, no, he's not.' 'Oh, yes, he is.' Such was Ned's certainty that the Bath selectors became convinced that he was right. Then Ned said, 'He's an undercover agent in the British Army – part of an elite squad – he's what's known as a shepherd spy!'

## Feet of clay

As Bath's rugby supremacy started to wane, Rowell recognised that some surgery was needed on the team and that one or two legends of the greatest team of all time needed to be put out to grass. Rowell approached Damian Hopley, the former England international and current chief executive of the Professional Rugby Players' Association, and said, 'You are one of the giants of the game. You have played a huge part in making Bath the greatest team of all time. A hundred years from now, people will still be talking about you.'

Hopley's chest puffed out with pride, but his expression changed as Rowell continued, 'I just don't know how we'd get on without you. But we're going to give it a try.'

## I can be your hero

Richard Hill, self-styled hard man of English back play in the 1980s, was known as 'Rouge Tête'. He tells a story about Stuart Barnes. Much of Barnes's international career was spent as a substitute for Rob Andrew. In fact, it is surprising that he never got the nickname 'the Judge', as he spent so much time on the bench.

Before succumbing to the lure of Sky TV, Barnes was the manager of a building society. He was in work one day as usual in his office in the centre of Bath. His three lady cashiers were working hard at the front desk and Stuart was keeping an eye on proceedings in his office with his two closed-circuit TV monitors. The ladies at the counter were suddenly confronted by a masked gunman, demanding money over the counter. The three women bravely tried to stall the gunman, playing for time. After all, they thought, the tough, brave England rugby player Mr Barnes would soon charge from his desk and rescue the three women in distress. They waited . . . and waited – but no sign of Barnes. They eventually had to give the gunman the money and he charged off. The cashiers were trembling after their traumatic ordeal and in a state of shock, but there was still no sign of Stuart. Where was their boss and hero? They found him not behind his desk but underneath it!

In 1990, after Bath beat old rivals Gloucester 6–3 in a closely fought match to reach the Pilkington Cup final, the Bath players and their significant others retreated to the Rec for a celebration after the game. Barnes was reportedly chatting with one of the supporters and offered to buy him a drink. 'What would you like?'

The fan thought he was in heaven, having a drink bought for him by the Bath captain, and replied, 'I'd like something tall, cold and full of gin.'

'Then come and meet my wife,' answered Barnes.

## Prop idol

Jack Rowell is renowned for his straight talking. He once described the former England prop Gareth Chilcott as 'green around the gills and a stranger to the lavatory'. He was also a hard taskmaster. Shortly after Chilcott got married, Rowell called his wife into the office. He instructed there was to be no lovemaking before the Pilkington Cup final and handed her a bottle of sleeping tablets to ensure that her husband had a quiet night. 'How many is he to take?' she asked.

'They're not for Gareth. They're for you,' he replied.

Chilcott was paid the supreme compliment by Bath and England hooker Graham Dawe when he called his prizewinning bullock on his farm in Devon 'Mr Chilcott'. Gareth's other nicknames were 'Coochie' and 'Oddjob' (after the Bond film character).

Gareth has a great sense of humour and a quick wit, but on the pitch he was not willing to take any form of intimidation, physical or verbal. All those qualities were evident in his memorable exchange with Wales's Dai Young: 'If you carry on niggling me, son, you're going to live up to your name.'

In the history of English rugby, there may have been greater players than Chilcott but there has never been a greater personality or storyteller. He knows it is better to tell an average story brilliantly than a brilliant story averagely, and Chilcott has a treasure trove of great stories about his involvement in the game. To add to his appeal, he has no problems telling stories that reflect badly on himself. He once described himself as 'looking like an 18-stone pear'.

At the height of his fame, he was invited to speak to the members of the Royal State Oil Club of Oman. It was to be a talk-and-leave arrangement. He would fly in for the function and fly straight back again. The problem was that his plane was delayed at Heathrow and he arrived at the airport in Oman just ten minutes before he was due to speak at the function. In a state of mild panic, he rushed for a taxi and asked how long it would take to get to the Royal State Oil Club. He was told it would take ten minutes. Chilcott breathed a huge sigh of relief and asked the taxi driver, 'There's a big entertainment function taking place there, can you take me, please?'

The taxi driver readily assented. With relief, Chilcott relaxed and, in the heat, fell asleep. When he woke up over an hour later, he was still in the taxi and the driver was still driving. He went into a total panic and shouted at the taxi driver, 'You told me it would only take ten minutes but we've been driving now for over an hour. Where the hell are you taking me?'

'You were looking for entertainment. I thought I'd take you

to a great club owned by my brother-in-law. It would be so much more fun than the Royal State Oil Club. Anyway, they've got that rugby player Gareth Chilcott speaking tonight. Can you imagine listening to anyone more boring?'

In a similar vein, Chilcott tells the story of his Bath teammate, Ben Clarke. After they won the Pilkington Cup final in 1994, some of the team visited a home for the elderly which offered specialist care to those suffering from senile dementia. Following the initial introductions, the players settled down to speak to individual residents. Clarke made polite conversation with a reserved-looking woman. It became clear that the woman didn't really understand what was happening and Clarke gently asked, 'Do you know who I am?'

The woman shook her head sadly and replied, 'No, but if you go and ask Matron, she'll tell you. She knows everyone in here.'

## Bop till you drop

Apart from Jack Rowell, England has produced a number of other top coaches. Geoff Cooke really paved the way for England to enter the professional era. The former English scrum-half Dewi Morris famously said, 'Geoff Cooke said that when he was finished with me I'd be fit to drop. I was and he did.'

Lock Nigel Redman recalls Cooke's unusual way of dropping him from the English team. He called Redman into his office at Twickenham, handed him a dice and told him to throw it on the desk, saying, 'Roll a one to five and you're dropped.'

'What if I get a six?' asked Redman.

'You get another throw.'

## Pin-up boy

Martin Bayfield won 61 England caps in the second row in the 1990s and toured with the Lions in 1993. Standing 6 ft 10 in.

in his socks, he was an unlikely sex symbol. By profession, Martin was once a policeman. During his days on the beat, he was taking part in the search of a known drug-dealer's house. The man was also known to be a homosexual. While searching downstairs, Martin heard roars of laughter from upstairs. His sergeant, with tears of mirth toppling in steady streams down his cheeks, came down to fetch him. There, above the man's bed, was a poster of Bayfield in all his glory.

Bayfield, like Gareth Chilcott before him, has gone on to have great success as an after-dinner speaker. One of his favourite stories is of an encounter in his playing days as an amateur with Dean Richards, a fellow policeman, in a club match. After Deano gave him a thump, Bayfield crumpled to the ground. Deano calmly remarked, 'You can tell which copper works behind a desk.'

## The man in the middle

Bob Hiller, the former England full-back, was playing for Harlequins and during the match was continually talking to the referee regarding the validity of his decisions. After Quins scored a try, Bob was preparing for the conversion and said something else to the ref. The ref had had enough by this stage and asked, 'Look here, Hiller, who's refereeing this match, me or you?'

Hiller replied, 'That's the problem, neither of us.'

Another story told about Hiller goes back to 1989 when England beat France 11–0 at Twickenham. Hiller was at the bar when he was approached by Dewi Morris. Part of Dewi's ritual after every international was to smoke a single cigarette, and he noticed Bob playing with a box of matches. 'May I have a light, please?' Dewi asked, holding up a cigarette.

'No,' replied Bob.

'You're Bob Hiller, aren't you?'

'Yes.'

'I always heard you were a really good bloke and I'm a bit

cheesed off with your attitude. I asked you politely for a light and although you have one you won't give it to me.'

'Ah, but refusing you a light shows just how caring I am.'

'I don't get you.'

'Well, if I gave you a light for that cigarette, you might feel obliged to offer me one and I'd smoke it. Then, when I lit up, I'd feel obliged to offer you one and we'd end up in conversation and offering one another cigarettes. Then you'd feel obliged to buy me a drink the next time you wanted a pint.'

'And what would be wrong with that?'

'Well, I'd then feel obliged to buy you a drink. Then you'd buy me one and so we'd go on all evening, buying each other drinks. Then, at the end of the night, you'd tell me you had nowhere to stay in London and, as we'd have spent the evening in one another's company, I'd feel compelled to invite you back to my home.'

'And would that be so terrible?'

'The problem is we only have two bedrooms. My wife and I sleep in one and my daughter sleeps in the other. She's almost 21 and every young man in the area thinks she looks like Miss World. You, being a typical rugger bugger, would give in to your animal instincts. Next thing you'd have her pregnant and you'd be telling me that you wouldn't stand by her.'

'But I would, I really would.'

'Well, you won't have to. You see, I'm not going to give you a light.'

## Speedie

The Wasps and England prop Paul Rendall was renowned for many aspects of forward play, but not for his speed. A feature of the build-up to any international that the 'Voice of Rugby' Bill McLaren was commentating on was that he would attend at least one training session of the two teams to familiarise himself with the players. Bill has a sweet tooth and always carried a tin of Hawick Balls with him. A 'sook' of these sweets was enjoyed by many a leading international. Once, he offered one to Paul Rendall and told him it would put a yard on his pace. In his best Slough accent, Paul replied, 'Well, in that case, you'd better give me the whole bleeding tin!'

It was said of Rendall that if he was any more laid back he would fall over. He did have a nice, dry sense of humour. He described his teammate Brian Moore thus: 'I think Brian's gnashers are the kind you get from a DIY shop and hammer in yourself. He is the only player we have who looks like a French forward.'

## Moore to the point

Brian Moore relished both the physical and psychological aspects of rugby. During one of the games on the Lions tour in 1993 he was rucking beside Nick Popplewell. Poppy got a blow to the head and said to Moore, 'I can see two balls, I can't continue.'

Moore replied, 'Get back on the pitch and kick both.'

Like Eric Cantona, Moore came up with some cryptic comments, notably, 'Anyone who is fully informed is totally confused.'

Moore was notorious for trying to outpsyche opponents before key internationals. Indeed some of his colleagues on the English team remarked that when he played against France in Paris he was more focused on putting his opponent off than playing his own game. There was one famous occasion when he was hoist with his own petard during Ireland's 13–12 win over England at Twickenham in 1994. The Irish players decided to start a fight with the English team early in the match to throw the English guys off their stride. In the dressing-room beforehand, the question arose as to who should start the fight. Everyone's eyes turned to Peter Clohessy. When the match started Clohessy was looking around for a suitable person to fight with. He first considered Jason Leonard, but he thought Leonard might be a bit of a handful to deal with, so his eyes fell on Brian Moore when there was a scrum in front of the English posts. Moore, like Peter Beardsley, is not the most handsome man in the world. One of his teammates said of him, in an alcohol-induced comment, that his front teeth are in the back of his mouth and his back teeth are in the front, and that he was born so ugly that his mother thought his face was on fire and she decided to put it out – with a shovel!

'The Claw' said to him, 'Listen, pal, what are you going to do for a face when Saddam wants his arsehole back?' Moore immediately started a bust-up and because he struck the first blow Ireland got a penalty and three easy points.

Moore appeared on a special edition of the popular quiz programme *The Weakest Link* in March 2004. The programme also featured France's Thomas Castaignede, Ireland's Geordan Murphy and England's Martin Bayfield and Will Greenwood. The programme is presented by England's most acerbic and ginger TV personality, Anne Robinson. In the chat between the questions Anne asked Brian what he would do if he were Prime Minister. Brian tactfully replied, 'I'd ban ginger people from being on television.'

However, it was Will Greenwood who got the biggest laugh when Anne asked him to explain the game of rugby. He replied, 'It's two teams of 15 a side who try to get a ball up the opposition's end.'

## Sacred writing

Forwards, affectionately of course, refer to backs as 'fairies'. In turn, backs refer to forwards as 'donkeys'. In Gloucester, though, the lines of demarcation are more clearly established. The Holy Writ of Gloucester Rugby Club demands: first, that the forwards shall win the ball; second, that the forwards shall keep the ball; and third, that the backs shall buy the beer.

## A travesty

In the dressing-room at Twickenham before the 1980 John Player Cup final, Peter Wheeler was rallying his Leicester troops. He told them they had to use all the possession they had to its full advantage, but not to do anything silly, because if the opposition tackled them early in the game and kicked the ball on to score, it would be a travesty. His tight-head prop Steve Redfern interjected, 'How many points will they get for a travesty?'

## Who am I?

Wasps were playing an unusually close derby game against their glamorous London rivals, Harlequins. Their regular scrum-half, Steve Bates, had cried off with an ankle injury on the morning of the game. As Wasps were experiencing a temporary shortage of scrum-halfs, they were forced to call up their fourth choice, Chris Wright. It was evident from an early stage that it was not going to be his day as nerves got the better of him. He was knocking balls on at the base of the scrum, and continually took the wrong option, much to the chagrin of his teammates. Just before half-time, as he made a break, Wright was at the wrong end of a crashing tackle by Peter Winterbottom. As he lay on the ground, groaning and groggy, the club physio, Sue Boardman, ran on to the field to treat him. After a few whiffs of the smelling salts, their scrum-half was still struggling to come to terms with his surroundings. Sue turned to the Wasps captain Dean Ryan and said, 'It's no good, Dean, he doesn't know who he is.'

After a short pause, Ryan replied, 'Then tell him he's Gareth Edwards.'

## Get smart

Strange things happen at rugby dinners. After an international against France in 1982, England's prop forward Colin Smart consumed a quantity of aftershave lotion at the post-match banquet in Paris. England's skipper and scrum-half Steve Smith commented, 'Colin may not have looked too good but he smelled lovely.'

Asked for his recollection of the evening the following day, Smart replied, 'It was about par for a rugby dinner, from what I can remember.'

Later in the season, when England beat Wales. Smith declared, 'The aftershave'll flow tonight.'

Steve Smith was not a man to let a good joke go easily. As he watched Smart showering himself in talcum powder after a subsequent match, Smith quipped, 'Nice to see you're back on solids, Smartie.'

## Yes, they call her the streak

Bill Beaumont was one of the most famous English and Lions second-rows. He has a nice line in self-deprecation: 'Playing in the second row doesn't require a lot of intelligence, really. You have to be bloody crazy to play there for a start.'

Despite winning 34 caps, captaining England to the 1980 Grand Slam and the Lions during their tour to South Africa in 1980, Bill's career is best remembered for an incident when he was giving a speech. England were playing Australia in 1982 and at half-time Bill had his back to the old South Stand at Twickenham. As he tried to rally the troops with his team talk, he noticed that he was gradually losing his colleagues' attention. Eventually, they were all peering over his shoulder, jostling to see what all the fuss was about. Rugby's most famous streaker, Erica Roe, was making her debut at Twickenham, racing across the pitch topless and injecting some much needed excitement into what had been a very dull game. Still, Bill held fast and did not turn around until Peter Wheeler shouted across, 'Bill, there's a bird just run on the park with your backside on her chest.'

Attending his first international that day was 11-year-old Matt Dawson. That was the day that Dawson decided he was going to become an England international. After winning the World Cup, he joked, 'I played for England so that I could be on the same pitch as Erica Roe. Instead, all I did was to get on the same pitch as Martin Johnson.'

In 1975, Beaumont won his second cap when he was forced to fill in at prop against Australia after only three minutes when Mike Burton was sent off. As a battered Beaumont made his way wearily back to the changing-room, he asked Fran Cotton what Burton was sent off for. Cotton replied, 'A late tackle.' Burton interjected, 'It couldn't have been that late, we'd only been playing three minutes.'

## Invincible

One of the jokes told about Bill Beaumont is that before England played New Zealand he was asked in a press conference: 'Some people think the All Blacks are invincible – does that worry you?'

'Of course it worries me if the All Blacks are invincible. I mean, it stands to reason, if we can't see them, how can we beat them?'

## Grammatically correct

Jack Rowell invited Bill Beaumont to speak at a Bath dinner. What did Bill do but tell a story about him? He said an American tourist had come up to Rowell in Bath and asked, ''Scuse me, where is the library at?'

Rowell allegedly made no effort to conceal the contempt in his voice when he answered, 'This is England. Here we speak the Queen's English. We do not end a sentence with a preposition.'

'OK,' said the tourist, 'where is the library at, asshole?'

## It's only words

Different personalities employ a wide variety of strategies to motivate teams. Phil Bennett psyched up his team against

England with the following oration: 'Look what these f**kers have done to Wales. They've taken our coal, our water, our steel, they buy our houses and they only live in them a fortnight every 12 months. What have they given us? Absolutely nothing. We've been exploited, raped, controlled and punished by the English – and that's who you are playing this afternoon.' Wales won handsomely.

England coach Dick Greenwood's speech to his team before their match against Australia was simply two words: 'England expects.' England lost 19–3.

Sometimes, though, Greenwood could get it spot on. The ex-England skipper's verdict on his first encounter with Wade Dooley was 'He was so big he blocked out the light.'

Dooley was not always so lucky. England captain Paul Dodge, introducing the debutant Dooley to the English team, said, 'Let's get right behind Wayne Gooley here.'

### Tunnel vision

The unexpected often happens in rugby. When England played Australia at Twickenham in 1984, they had to play for 13 minutes with only 14 players when Steve Mills got injured, as his replacement Steve Brain couldn't get on to the pitch because the tunnel doors were locked.

### Hair-raising

In 1980, when Ireland played England, Freddie McLennan and John Carleton were having a real jousting match. At one stage, John sent Freddie crashing to the ground in a tackle. As he was going back to his position, Freddie shouted at him, 'John! John! Is my hair all right?' The video of the game shows John cracking up with laughter and Freddie straightening his hair.

### Nice guy

Tony Neary was a star forward for England in the 1970s. Unlike many of his teammates, Tony preferred to be true to himself and show friendship rather than trying to outpsyche his opponents before big games.

In 1974, Ireland faced England at Twickenham. Before the game the Irish players were running onto the pitch when they were stopped in the tunnel by an official in a blazer, who had the archetypal RAF moustache. He said, 'Hang on, boys, the BBC cameras are not ready for you yet.' The Irish lads were just itching to get on the pitch and found the waiting a pain, particularly when they were joined in the tunnel by the English team. The English were led by their captain, John Pullin, who was shouting at his team about Waterloo. The Irish players couldn't understand what Waterloo had to do with them. The English players looked bigger and stronger than their Irish counterparts. As they were always on television, they were all huge stars, and they had mega names like David Duckham and Andy Ripley. The Irish players were studiously trying to avoid eye-contact with them because they planned to rough them up a bit on the pitch. However, Tony Neary went over and tapped Moss Keane on the shoulder and said, 'Moss, best of luck. May the best team win.'

Keane growled back, 'I f\*\*king hope not!'

His wish came true. Although they were the underdogs, Ireland won 26–21.

## The boxer

One of the most famous tours in rugby history was that of the Lions to South Africa in 1974. The tour saw some very physical exchanges on the pitch. One of the props on the tour, Gloucester's Mike Burton, was well able to look after himself in these situations. The following year he became the first England international to be sent off in a Test match, following a clash with Australian winger Doug Osbourne. In the canon of rugby literature, Burton's autobiography *Never Stay Down* stands out. He devotes a chapter to the best punches he encountered in his career!

# England's Ruck and Rollers

## Bad tackle

Down through the years England has produced many players who were very difficult to tackle because of their speed, swerve or sidestep, or a combination of all three. Phil Horrocks-Taylor, though, was a special case. After a game against Ireland, his direct opponent Mick English described his botched efforts to put in a proper tackle on the Englishman: 'Every time I went to tackle him, Horrocks went one way, Taylor the other, and all I got was the bloody hyphen.'

## Country matters

In 1966, David Powell won his first cap for England. The prop earned his living as a farmer. When he heard about his call-up, he told his dad, who asked, 'Where's the match?'

Thinking that his dad might like to travel to the game, David replied, 'It's at home at Twickenham against Wales.'

'That's good,' his father said, 'you'll only want Saturday afternoon off work. Oh, and as it's a home game, you'll be able to milk the cows that morning and of course Sunday morning too.'

## Money's too tight to mention

The transition from amateurism to professionalism in 1995 proved problematic in every rugby country. At the time, a RFU official on BBC Radio Five Live said, 'You ask me if headquarters worry about change. Well, hardly – everything is paid for by cheque.'

It was not always thus. Following his late call-up to the England squad in 1991, Damian Hopley said, 'When I heard that the Rugby Union were on the line, I thought it might be a query about my expenses!'

Carston Catcheside played in an era when the Headingly RFC crest motto *Ludlum non victoriam amare* (love the game, not victory) was an ideal the top players aspired to. He won eight caps between 1924 and 1927. He is one of an elite group:

those who have scored a try in each of four international championship matches in the Five Nations. He submitted a £3 expense claim to cover the cost of a Newcastle–London trip. However, the RFU treasurer deducted a penny because he knew that Carston had 'rounded up' his bill. In response, Catcheside submitted a more detailed breakdown:

Fare £2 19s 11d. Toilet 1d. Total £3.

In his later years, one of Carston's more difficult tasks was to keep himself updated on the changing rugby vocabulary. One time he was watching *Rugby Special* and he heard a guest talking about an 'executive high ball'. He asked a few people later if they knew what that was. Eventually, he learned that it was the new name for the garryowen!

### French kissing

Former English international open-side flanker Richard Pool-Jones played most of his club rugby in France. He recalled a clash between clubs from France and England where the exchanges were particularly savage. After the match, the French and English hookers decided to heal the wounds by having a bottle of wine together. It was an occasion of turning wine into water. After one bottle became five, the Frenchman couldn't resist boasting to his new English friend, 'Deed you know, een ma coontry, we 'ave 101 ways of making love?'

The English player was dumbstruck and feebly confessed: 'That's astonishing! In England, we only have one.'

The Frenchman asked quizzically: 'Ah yes? And wat wood zat be?'

The Englishman said: 'Well, there's a man and a woman, and . . .'

'Mon Dieu!' shouted the Frenchman. 'Number 102!'

### Man of the Year

One lesson every player has to learn is never to take themselves too seriously. A few years ago when *Rugby Special* were doing their review of the year they asked rugby correspondent Stephen Jones to select his Man of the Year. He went back to England's victory over Australia. The crucial point in the match came when an Australian try was disallowed because the 'scorer' had put his foot in touch. Until people saw the TV replay it was difficult to be certain that it was the correct decision. The linesman who made the decision that day was Stephen Hilditch. He was watching *Rugby Special* at home and got very excited when he heard all the praise he was receiving and as they were preparing to announce Man of the Year he rushed off to get his wife. Just as she ran in, they announced the winner – it was the cameraman who proved Stephen's decision was the right one.

## No sound and vision

The presenter of BBC's *Rugby Special*, John Inverdale, did not have the most auspicious beginning to his career in broadcasting. He had to interview the 'Voice of Boxing', Harry Carpenter, for BBC radio. Inverdale was so nervous that during the interview he failed to notice that he hadn't put a tape in his tape recorder.

## Up-Hill struggle

Nigel Starmer-Smith is one of the great institutions of English rugby. As a former English international himself, Nigel became one of the great rugby commentators with the BBC. There was the odd moment, though, when his achievements did not get the credit they deserved. One example was when his BBC colleague, Jimmy Hill, introduced him as 'a man who has seven craps as scrum-half for England'.

Nigel himself had the odd blip in the commentary box, notably: 'If you didn't know him, you wouldn't know who he was.'

## Revenge of the jokers

For years, English players were the butt of Irish jokes. More recently, though, the English lads have started taking their revenge. The pioneer was Jeff Probyn, who said, 'The Irish treat you like royalty before and after a game, and kick you to pieces during it.'

Invariably in recent years, the prime target has been Keith Wood. Wade Dooley tells the story of Ireland touring Japan when the team hotel was destroyed by a massive earthquake. While searching the rubble, the local police heard a faint voice from under the debris: 'It's Keith Wood, the Irish captain. Is anyone there?'

'Keith. Keep talking. Where are you? We're going to get you out.'

'Yes, it's me. I can hear you. I'm OK. I'm in room 247.'

English winger Dan Luger tells a story about a man who loved his garden in the days when Woodie was an amateur. One day his world almost ended when he woke up to see that his pride and joy was scarred by a proliferation of molehills. He was distraught, but soon wiped away his tears, got out the Yellow Pages and saw an ad which read 'For the best mole-catcher in town, call Keith Wood – simply the best'.

Woodie's days as a rugby pro were still ahead of him and he was on the job instantly. He promised the man he would solve the problem. He stood on watch all night hoping to catch the mole but with no luck. The next night he repeated the vigil but again there was no sign of the mole. By now the garden-owner was irate and said to Wood, 'When you catch this damned mole, make him die the worst death you can imagine – really nasty.'

The next morning Wood was jubilant, 'I caught him, just as I promised.'

'That's wonderful news. How did you kill him?'

'Horribly,' replied Woodie. 'I buried him alive.'

In reply, Wood tells the story of the Irishman who

approached an English foreman for work on a building site. The latter fancied himself as a great wit. 'What's your name, Paddy?' he enquired of the Irish chap. 'Michael Moran,' came the reply.

'Anything to do with the Mountains of Mourne?' the wit asked.

'No, but my mother was one of the Hills of Donegal.'

Unusual fuel was added to the fire of Anglo–Irish relations during the Lions tour to Australia in 2001. After an exhausting training session, Rob Henderson was fast asleep on the team bus on the seat by the loo. Lawrence Dallaglio was in the loo doing his business. Unfortunately, he neglected to lock the door properly and when the driver suddenly braked hard he was hurled out the door literally in full flow. Sadly, Henderson was in the wrong place at the wrong time and had the English forward's urine raining down on him. Woken up by a combination of the ensuing laughter and a feeling of dampness, Hendo said, 'What the hell is this? I'm really pissed off.'

A chorus came up from the bus, 'Hendo, you've also been pissed on.'

To his credit, one man who is above all this is Stuart Barnes. The former England and Lions fly-half is now a Sky TV commentator and analyst. During an England–Ireland game, Sky's chief commentator, Miles Harrison, remarked, 'Wood has been penalised for going down on the England hooker.'

Barnes intervened immediately: 'No, that's terrible, you cannot go down on a hooker on the field of play, Miles!'

## Hand-y work

Female rugby players face different sorts of problems in the scrum. English ladies' rugby captain Emma Mitchell answered the question, wouldn't women rugby players be vulnerable to breast damage? 'The way you are taught to take contact in rugby is with your shoulder, leaning forward. This means that the most vulnerable part is protected. And, anyway, I'd argue that men are much more vulnerable to . . . underhand tactics, shall we say.'

## Horse sense

Jason Leonard tells the story of a former scrum-half who, although he was married, had a roving eye. The player in question was sitting at home quietly one evening reading his newspaper when his wife sneaked up behind him and whacked him around the head with a frying pan. 'What was that for?' he asked.

'I was doing your washing for you and while I was going through your trouser pockets I found a piece of paper with the name Sandra on it and a number after it.'

'Don't be so stupid,' he said. 'Two weeks ago I backed a horse called Sandra and she won. The number was my bookie's. You remember when I brought you home those dozen roses? Well, I bought them with my winnings. I'm sorry now I bothered.'

'Oh, darling, I'm so sorry. How can you ever forgive me?'

The next evening the player was again at home reading his paper. Again his wife sneaked up behind him and whacked him on the head with the frying pan, this time knocking him out cold.

When he came around, he asked again: 'What was that for?'

His wife answered through gritted teeth, 'Your f**king horse phoned.'

# TWO

# Flower of Scotland

### Logan's run

Apart from being husband to popular TV presenter Gabby, Kenny Logan is one of Scotland's most capped internationals. He tells a story which highlights his sometimes strained relations with the Scottish fans. Scotland were playing England in a Grand Slam decider. A Scottish fan was watching the match in a pub in Edinburgh with a row of whiskies and his faithful terrier named Thistle. England had possession, their big ugly pack rumbled towards the halfway line, then eventually gave the ball to the scrum-half. He booted it upfield. Kenny Logan caught the ball on the wing. He began to run but, seeing a wall of Englishmen charging towards him, stopped, took aim and struck over a beautiful drop-goal. The Scotsman in the pub threw his arms in the air, Thistle the dog jumped up on the bar, got up on his hind legs, did a double back-flip somersault, a quick breakdance routine and then slammed down two of the whiskies.

'Bloody hell, mate,' said the barman, 'that's incredible, he only kicked a drop-goal. What happens when Logan scores a try?'

'I dunno,' replied the Scotsman. 'I've only had him for four years.'

### The three musketeers

During the 1999 World Cup, boredom spread in the Scottish camp. Tom Smith, Scott Murray and Martin Leslie were desperately seeking a diversion. Gregor Townsend was to provide them unwittingly with exactly the distraction they craved. At the time, Reebok had a huge campaign going across the UK, using various players who were starring in the World Cup. In Wales, there were huge posters of Rob Howley around: 'Rob Howley wears Reebok, Howley the Whirlwind.' Scotland's hero Townsend was similarly immortalised: 'Gregor Townsend wears Reebok, Townsend the Timebomb.' The three musketeers felt obliged to take Townsend down a peg or two. Every opportunity they got and every venue they entered, from restaurants to post offices, they put up their own Townsend poster which read rather differently: 'Gregor Townsend wears suspenders, Townsend the Cross-dresser.'

Townsend was furious. One day the troublesome threesome decided to take their campaign a step further. They 'borrowed' four A3 sheets from the tactics flip chart and composed the biggest and most impressive ad campaign for Gregor to date. They sellotaped their poster to the side of the bus stop up the road. Shortly after, the squad were being driven by coach to training and they passed the bus stop. They were all in stitches when they saw that the whole bus stop was taken up by the ad campaign stating: 'Gregor Townsend wears suspenders,

Townsend the Cross-dresser.' Gregor screamed at the driver to stop the bus and ran out and tore it down.

Later that evening, a journalist got wind of the story and asked the three musketeers what they really thought of Townsend. They said, 'Och, Gregor is a grand wee chappie, though it's said that he accepts lavish compliments as readily as toast accepts butter. He never, ever says a bad word about anyone. He's too busy talking about himself!'

## Rob the ditherer

No international coaching partnership is more respected than Ian 'Geech' McGeechan and Jim Telfer. That reputation was enhanced still further with their great success on the Lions tour to South Africa in 1997. The type of totally committed and dedicated player they sought was encapsulated in the Scottish forward Rob Wainwright. Telfer was preparing the team for the match against the Cats in Johannesburg. The forwards had already been working intensely for an hour and were on the brink of total exhaustion. Telfer was turning redder and redder from shouting at them to give even more. Jim decided they were going to do a rucking drill, so all the forwards gathered behind the ball-carrier to face the pads for rucking drills. Wainwright was appointed ball-carrier. Off the forwards trouped. Wainwright crashed into the first pad and dropped the ball.

Telfer went apoplectic: 'You f**king idiot, get back to the start.'

The forwards went back to their places. Once more into the breach, and again Wainwright dropped the ball. Telfer went demented.

Third time lucky? No chance. Wainwright again dropped the ball. There was a collective intake of breath. What would Telfer say next? They didn't have long to wait: 'Wainwright, bloody Wainwright. You're like a lighthouse in the desert . . . brilliant but f**king useless.'

## Period of adjustment

Confusion was not something Ian McGeechan ever tolerated. He is universally recognised as one of the great coaches in the history of world rugby. He was an innovator and never shy about using new methods. Occasionally he recognised that change brought teething problems: 'Like women, different scrummaging machines can take some getting used to.'

Even in a crisis he was always able to keep a cool head and see the humour in difficult situations. In 1991, after Derek White had eight 'staples' inserted in a head wound during the international trial, McGeechan said, 'He's all right but he'll not be able to go through any airport security scanners for a while.'

McGeechan, though, was no shrinking violet when it came to instructing his players to tough it out when confronted with serious opposition – particularly if the headline in *The Sun* on Derek Turnbull's inclusion in the Scotland team to meet France in 1991 was true: 'Turnbull Told: Flatten Frogs'.

Turnbull had been a sub against France in Paris in 1989. Asked about his experience during the game, Turnbull replied, 'All I did really was listen to the band.'

In 1994, McGeechan was appointed coach at Northampton. During his first coaching session at Franklin's Gardens he reactivated an old injury from his distinguished playing career, which saw him win 32 caps for Scotland. When he went into the physio's room, only the club captain Tim Rodber was present. 'Do you have anything for this old rugby knee?' asked the new coach.

Rodber replied, 'Only the greatest respect.'

## Matt-er-of-fact

With the retirement of McGeechan after the 2003 World Cup, Australian Matt Williams was appointed Scottish coach, having had great success with Leinster. He should have known the magnitude of the task when BBC commentator Nick Mullins noted that his selection was akin to 'rearranging deckchairs on the *Titanic*'.

Williams is one of the increasing number of coaches who have made the journey from down under to Britain and Ireland, having begun his coaching career with New South Wales. Williams once described the cultural differences between Ireland and France. 'In Ireland, they take you to parties and give you loads of free drink in the pubs and then kick the daylights out of you on the pitch. They do the same in France except they don't take you to parties or give you free drink in the pubs.'

Before Matt Williams was sacked as Scottish coach in April 2005, many people in Scottish rugby were unhappy with the growing influence of Aussies on the Scottish game, not just at coaching level but also amongst the playing community. The former Scottish international John Beattie jokes that such is the current Aussie influence on Scottish rugby, Murrayfield will have to be rechristened 'Ramsay Street' after the celebrated street in Australia's most famous soap, *Neighbours*.

## Banana sprints

In 1997, France faced Scotland in a Grand Slam decider. Before the match, the crowd were treated to a strange sight. The French always had bananas available for the players at training. The Monday before the game, their prop, Christian Califano, decided to have one. There was no bin nearby so he dumped the skin in Olivier Merle's boots when the big man's back was turned. As Merle stands 6 ft 6 in. tall in his bare feet, this was a brave move. To Califano's surprise there was no reaction all week from Merle. What the prop didn't realise was that his teammate had two pairs of boots: one pair for training and another, special pair he only wore for matches. Califano had used the match boots as his personal rubbish bin. The problem was, nobody else realised this. Everybody assumed he had found the boots and just not mentioned the offending fruit. Meanwhile the banana skin continued to fester and congeal in

Merle's left boot. Before the match, the French players went out onto the pitch, warmed up and then went back into the changing-room. Minutes before kick-off, they were all concentrating when there was a huge roar. It was Merle, who had finally put on his boots and his foot had come into contact with a sticky, smelly mess.

Califano turned a whiter shade of pale and immediately went to apologise. Merle was not for placating and, in a fit of rage, started chasing Califano around the dressing-room. Their teammates intervened, shouting the French equivalent of 'We've a game in five minutes.' The Scottish fans thought how pumped up the two protagonists were, sprinting onto the pitch at a pace that brought back memories of Carl Lewis and Ben Johnson. They didn't understand that Merle was running on rage and Califano on pure fear.

## Chinese whispers

One of Scotland's most famous captains, Gavin Hastings, sustained an ankle injury in an international in 1990. He was asked how he was feeling. He replied, 'Well, I'll certainly not be doing the lambada tonight.'

Such is the fame of Hastings, the scorer of 667 points in 61 Tests for Scotland, that he was invited to give a training session to the Chinese rugby team. The team consisted largely of army personnel. Accordingly, the People's Liberation Army invited a British TV crew to film the proceedings. It was a major departure to allow the cameras into the notoriously secretive army fortress. Much to the crew's astonishment the Chinese bent over backwards to facilitate the recording. Nothing was too much trouble. No request was too unreasonable. Everything was going swimmingly until . . .

To round off the programme the director thought it would be nice to finish with a shot that would highlight the contrast between the old repressive China and the new modern one that the rugby team represented. Beside the rugby pitch was a naff old wall, with Chinese writing on it. In the evening light, the director would get the players to stand in front of the wall, wearing their bright new international shirts, in marked contrast to the faded, crumbling wall behind them, and get them to cheer. As soon as he mentioned this brainwave to the coach and players, the atmosphere changed dramatically. He was puzzled by their sudden undisguised hostility and sought to get the interpreter to intercede on his behalf. When he explained the plan, the interpreter turned pale and gulped. 'You want the Chinese national team to stand in front of that wall, under that writing, and cheer?'

'What's so wrong with that?'

'That wall was the firing squad wall, and the writing translated means "All traitors of the People's Republic of China stand here and die".'

For some reason, the People's Republic of China have never presented Gavin Hastings with any of their official awards to distinguished visitors.

## The language of love

In 1995, Scotland beat France in Paris for the first time in 30 years. Scotland's win had been sealed when Gavin Hastings had sprinted in for a 40-metre try under the posts. The French held a magnificent banquet afterwards in a very palatial setting. To reciprocate the French grace in defeat, Hastings decided that he would give his speech in French. There was a trifling obstacle to be overcome first. He hadn't a word of French. He decided to recruit the services of Damian Cronin, who had played club rugby in France for a couple of seasons. He asked Cronin to translate. He was a little concerned that his opening was too banal. His first two sentences were: 'Ladies and gentlemen, it gives me great pleasure to stand before you. I thank you for your kind hospitality after a mad, passionate game.' As soon as he said these words he was totally stunned by the reaction. The French contingent gave him a standing ovation and almost broke the sound barrier with their fierce clapping and cheering. Hastings couldn't fathom what he had done to elicit such a rapturous response. It was later in the evening that he discovered that Cronin had translated his sentences as: 'Ladies and gentlemen, it gives me great pleasure to tell you that as soon as I finish this speech I am looking forward to taking my wife upstairs and having mad, passionate sex with her!'

## Great expectations

Gavin Hastings was a prolific penalty kicker but even the very best can have an off-day. In 1991, England travelled to Murrayfield to play Scotland in the World Cup semi-final. Having beaten the Auld Enemy so memorably to claim the Grand Slam the year before, Scottish rugby was on a high. The entire nation was gripped by the semi-final and had great expectations of winning. In an incredibly close contest, the match was tied at 6–6 when late in the game Scotland got an easy penalty right in front of the posts. Everyone in the ground was certain Gavin would slot it over to put Scotland in the ascendancy. The kick, incredibly, drifted high but to the right. Rob Andrew got a late drop-goal to give England a 9–6 victory. After the game, in the dressing-room Gavin said, 'Sorry for missing that penalty kick. I don't know what went wrong – it was such an easy shot. I could kick myself.'

David Sole is reputed to have said acidly, 'I shouldn't bother. You'd probably miss!'

## Sole mates

David Sole was both a wonderful loose-head prop and captain for Scotland. He will always be remembered for marching, instead of running, the Scottish team onto the field before the 1990 Grand Slam decider in a grimly determined gesture.

At the height of his career he was being interviewed for a local radio station. He was asked on what side he played in the scrum. In his best Scottish accent he jokingly replied, 'Sometimes I play on the right side, sometimes I play on the left side – but not right and left at the same time!'

## Brothers in arms

Tony Stanger guaranteed his immortality by scoring that famous try against England in the Grand Slam decider in 1990. During the 2003 World Cup, he was having a quiet drink when an elderly man was introduced to him. The old man asked him to sign an autograph for his seven grandsons. Out of the blue he asked Tony: 'Who were that great pair who I used to love watching playing for bonnie Scotland?'

After pausing for thought, Stanger suggested John Rutherford and Roy Laidlaw.

'Nay, laddie, two brothers, they are. Gavin Hastings and Scott . . . Scott, am, am, Scott. . . Good God, what's the bloke's surname?'

'Hastings.'

'Och, that's it. Thanks, ma laddie. I've been trying to think of his name for days now.'

## A royal occasion

Rugby is a game where sportsmanship is always to the fore. During the 2003 World Cup semi-final, Australian prop Ben Darwin sustained a serious neck injury, which ended his career. Darwin credits the All Black prop Kees Meeuws with saving his life. When the scrum went down in that game, Darwin shouted 'neck, neck, neck' and the All Blacks immediately stopped pushing.

It will surprise outsiders to discover that etiquette is also at the heart of rugby. Before Scotland played England in the Grand Slam decider in 1990, the teams were presented to the Royal party, consisting of Princess Anne and her two young children Peter and Zara Phillips. One of the Scottish players unfortunately 'blew wind' at just the wrong moment. After the game and Scotland's incredible win, one might have expected the backroom team to be thrilled. However, one of them went up to the player with too much fibre in his diet and said, 'You've let us all down. Don't you know you can't fart before royalty?'

The player was very contrite. 'I'm so sorry. I had no idea Princess Anne wanted to fart first.'

### Ooouch!

It was pretty obvious who the Royal party wanted to win before the match, as Princess Anne was wearing tartan, as were her two children who were following behind, shaking hands as well. As Will Carling had almost finished introducing the party to the English team, there was an unmerciful scream. Wade Dooley had squeezed little Peter Phillips' hand during the handshake. Dooley was the first Englishman to get stuck into a Scot that day.

### The White Shark

One Scottish player always up for taking on any opposition was J.J., aka John Jeffrey. There are a lot of stories told about the 'White Shark'. The veracity of some of them is highly questionable. One of the ones that has a ring of strange-but-untrue starts with him watching an international between Wales and Romania on the television with Finlay Calder. Wales had most of the play but for some inexplicable reason kept dropping the ball near the try-line. According to folklore, Jeffrey turned around and said to Calder, 'The Welsh must have dropped the ball at least five times today with the try-line at their mercy.'

Calder is said to have replied: 'Oh no, it's more than that. I'd put it into double figures. I think they've dropped the ball *nine* times already.'

A variation of the story has Calder saying: 'Gavin Hastings has kicked 43 goals this season so far. That's exactly twice as many as last year.'

# Flower of Scotland

## Braveheart

Finlay Calder made a massive contribution to the Scottish pack. He was a very strong player yet very physically mobile about the pitch. The former Scottish captain was a joker who practised a fascinating combination of fun-poking, often at himself, and reasoned judgement.

At one post-international press conference he added a caveat when confirming that the Scottish squad would attend the official dinner as normal: 'Unless Jim Telfer decides to have a rucking session on the way up the Bridges.'

In 1989, annoyed by Dean Richards' ability to stem the flow of opposition ruck ball, he said, 'Aye, that Dean Richards is an awful laddie – he deserves a good howkin'.'

Calder never shied away from giving an honest opinion. In 2001, he was asked his opinion about Iain Balshaw, who had just made his breakthrough in the Six Nations. He replied, 'If Iain Balshaw is an international full-back, then I'm Mel Gibson.'

## Impressing the natives

When Liverpool legend Ian Rush was transferred to Juventus, he famously said, 'Going to Italy is like moving to a different country.' When a centre from New Zealand, Sean Lineen, declared for Scotland in 1989, he was flown to his grandfather's birthplace in Stornoway. He had qualified to play for Scotland under the grandparentage rule. Before he left, the ever helpful Finlay Calder and John Jeffrey told him they only spoke Gaelic on the island, and they even gave him some 'good phrases' to use. Determined to make a good impression as soon as he arrived at Stornoway, Lineen went on a charm offensive by addressing the assembled media and islanders at the airport in Gaelic. He expected to be onto a winner when he said: '*Pòg m'hone*.' From Jeffrey and Calder he had learned this meant 'This is a lovely island and I'm really looking forward to meeting everyone.' He was shocked that his remark was met with glacial silence and angry looks.

He subsequently discovered that the phrase actually meant 'Kiss my arse!'

Lineen struggled to get up to speed on Scottish accents. A Scottish fan with a strong brogue approached Lineen in the bar after a match against South Africa and congratulated him on his performance. Lineen replied, 'Sorry, mate, I don't speak Afrikaans.'

## Peaches and cream

In the 1980s, Scotland had a dream half-back combination of Roy Laidlaw and 'Gentleman' John 'Rud' Rutherford. Laidlaw struck up an instant rapport with his half-back partner on and off the field. It was said that they went together like ham and eggs, and that Laidlaw could find Rutherford in a darkened room. The scrum-half was heard to proclaim that Rutherford was not the first person he would want to meet in those circumstances.

## Mistaken identity

For some reason, confusion appears to reign at all levels of Scottish rugby:

English official at a post-match dinner: 'The soup was tepid.'

The Scottish 1984 Grand Slam lock Alister Campbell: 'I thought it was chicken!'

A more painful form of culinary mistaken identity took place during a Scottish tour of Japan. Scottish prop Gerry McGuinness was asked, following his release from hospital, to explain why he had eaten lotus-leaf garnish. He replied, 'Listen, pal, where I come from, you eat everything that's put down in front of you.'

During a trial in Jedburgh Sheriff Court, a barrister cross-examined a youth about a brawl between some Kelso youths and a local gang of motorbikers called the Barbarians: 'Do you know any Barbarians?'

The witness replied, 'Yes, John Jeffrey.'

A Kelso forward was asked how his bad back was. He replied, 'It's a lot better. I've been to see a chiropodist.' In fact he had consulted a chiropractor!

### Don't look now

Scottish captains tend to be very single-minded and constantly exhort their colleagues to adopt similar tunnel vision. Their Grand Slam skipper Jim Aitken was giving his half-time team talk at Twickenham in 1983 when two buxom streakers graced the pitch. Aitken said, 'Don't look, boys. Concentrate on the game. There'll be plenty of time for that later.'

Aitken sometimes didn't quite have the best of luck with his motivational speeches. Before playing England he said, according to folklore, 'There are two things to remember today, men. First, there is going to be only one team out there today. How many teams will there be out there, then, lads?'

Everyone roared enthusiastically: 'ONE TEAM.'

'Second, just remember this. It's going to be the day when the men get sorted out from the boys. What's going to happen, lads?'

To a man the team chorused: 'ONE TEAM. MEN VERSUS BOYS.'

A minute later the referee popped his head into the dressing-room and said, 'Come on, boys. It's time to go.'

### The Voice

The Voice of Rugby Bill McLaren's own rugby-playing career with Hawick came to an abrupt end in October 1948 when it emerged that he had contracted tuberculosis of the lungs. As a player, McLaren was no shrinking violet. His father delighted in recalling an incident when he was watching his son play against Kelso and was seated beside a large farmer supporting Kelso. Outraged by Bill's robust tactics, the farmer referred to 'that big, dirty, black-headed bugger, McLaren'. Discretion was the better part of valour and Bill's dad decided that this was not the right moment to proudly profess the familial connection.

Bill is a master of self-deprecation. During the 1987 World Cup, he introduced his wife, Bette, to leading rugby administrator Syd Millar. Syd took one look at Bill, one at Bette and then said, 'Ah, Jaisus, Bette, you could have done a hell of a sight better!'

Bill's favourite quip, though, is Mick Quinn's whenever a young lady is introduced to him: 'Ah, hello again. How are ye? Oi didn't recognise you wit' yer clothes on!'

Loved universally wherever he toured, not surprisingly Bill was a big hit when he travelled to the home of Irish rugby, Limerick, for the Terry Wogan Golf Classic in 1991. The only problem was that when Terry Wogan made his speech to the crowd he said that, being a Scot, Bill McLaren was unlikely to throw his ball to the crowd at the end of the round.

McLaren's ode to a young Boroughmuir prop forward with a muscular physique was, 'He's built like a young bull.' He also had a nice euphemism for kicking a player – 'illegal use of the boot'.

Medics were consulted when, before the 2003 World Cup, Bill was heard to say, 'Scotland for the World Cup.' Their diagnosis was 'a nasty case of premature e-jock-ulation'.

Asked by this writer to tell his favourite story, Bill recalled the build-up to a Scotland v. Wales match in 1962. The day before the game, the leader of the Scottish pack, Hugh Ferns McLeod, was giving his team talk. He was a reluctant leader because he wanted to concentrate on his own job as a prop but once he was persuaded to take on the role by a Scottish selector, Alf Wilson, he wanted to do it properly. As he was speaking, he noticed the forwards, weren't paying attention and were talking among themselves. He was 5 ft 10 in. tall and he walked up to the forwards, who were all towering over him. Undaunted, Hugh said, 'Come here, ma wee disciples.' When they all gathered around, he continued, 'Now, Ah want tae tell ye that Ah've been asked tae lead this pack tomorrow. Ah'm no very keen on the job but that's what Ah'm going tae do and if any of you lot want to be pack-leader, just let me know and Ah'll put a word in for you at the right place. But the next one who opens his trap, Ah'll bring my boot right at his arse.'

One of the Anglo-Scots in the group said, 'Well, I didn't understand a word of that but it all sounded damned impressive.' They listened, and the next day beat the Welsh off the park, their first win in Wales for 25 years and their first win in Cardiff for 35 years.

Bill also tells the story of another of Hugh's motivational speeches. It came the following year, before Scotland played France in Paris. Hugh went up to his fellow forward Frans ten Bos and said, 'Frans, ye think ye're a guid forrit but really ye're jist a big lump o' potted meat. Ah'm goin' tae tell ye somethin'. If Ah was half yer size, Ah'd pick up the first two Frenchmen that looked at me the morn and Ah'd chuck them right over the bloody stand.' The next day Frans had the game of his life and Scotland won by 11 points to 6.

Bill claims that one of his most embarrassing moments came before commentating on England v. France in 1983. France had two locks new to the Championship in Jean Condom and Jean-Charles Orso. While it was a relief to discover that Condom pronounced his name 'Condong', Bill jokes that the embarrassment came in discovering what a condom was!

He is delighted, though, that he never made a faux pas comparable to those of his BBC colleagues Peter West and Bob Wilson. Commentating on Wimbledon, West said: 'Bjorn Borg, the top wanking Swede.' Wilson's misfortune was to say, 'News just through from Elland Road that Joe Jordan has just pissed a late fatness test.'

In 1973, France played England at Twickenham. Before the match, McLaren was asked on *Grandstand*'s preview what he thought of Fran Cotton. Bill replied, 'I haven't seen the big lad play yet but I had dinner with the England party last night and I saw Fran deal with a five-course dinner. He was very impressive indeed!'

There are three kinds of people in this world: those who can count and those who can't. Bill sometimes struggled with maths, 'That could have made it 10–3, and there's a subtle difference between that and 7–3.'

## Jim'll fix it

As well as being the Voice of Rugby, Bill's other profession was as a PE teacher at Drumlanrig St Cuthbert's Primary School in Hawick. His most famous pupil was former Scottish and Lions centre, Jim Renwick. When Bill retired from teaching in 1988, Jim was invited to make the presentation. The event was covered by BBC television. The interviewer asked Jim, 'Do you think that you would have gained 52 caps if you had not been coached by Bill McLaren?'

Jim paused theatrically. 'I think I would have got 70 caps if I hadn't been coached by Bill McLaren.'

In 1984, Scotland toured Romania. At the time things were pretty bleak behind the Iron Curtain and the Scottish team were in dire straits food-wise. Bill McLaren was due to travel out to see them play and Renwick contacted him to urge him to bring out food for the Scottish team. Bill nervously packed tins of sausages, beans, corned beef and powdered milk, as well as Mars bars in his bag, knowing that he would be in serious trouble if the customs authorities in Romania, a group of men not known for their understanding or sympathy, caught him out. When he got to Bucharest airport, Bill was approached by two burly security men who would have scared Hannibal Lecter and was told to step aside. Bill could hear the clang of the cell door closing. He was already visualising himself in a starring role in scenes from the film *Midnight Express*.

A long time passed as Bill waited in terror. Then it emerged that the problem was not his luggage but his passport. His passport described him as a teacher of physical education, whereas in the document he had filled in on the flight over he had described himself as a television commentator. Eventually the confusion was resolved and Bill's frayed nerves were finally soothed once he got outside the airport. He went straight to the Scottish team's hotel and gave Jim the food. The next day Jim thanked him for the food. When Bill asked if it had been well received, Jim replied, 'Oh, it was grand. They were so hungry they ate the tins as well!'

When Doddie Weir suggested to Jim before Scotland took on the might of the English pack that 'The bigger they are they harder they fall,' Renwick replied, 'Wrong. The bigger they are the harder they hit you.'

Jim had a good line in sarcasm. After Bruce Hay, who was not known for his speed, scored a try for Scotland he said, 'That's the first time I've seen a try scored live and in slow motion at the same time.'

Renwick was not the only one to come down hard on the Lions player. Hay was presented to the Duke of Edinburgh before a match, who said, 'And which lamppost did you bump into?'

In fairness to Renwick, he could also tell stories against himself. After he dropped a series of passes in an international, he was greeted by a Scotland fan who asked Renwick if he could shake hands with him. After the handshake took place, the fan said, 'Oh, so you have got hands after all.'

## A touch of class

Renwick's teammate Andy Irvine was one of the most thrilling players ever to play rugby. He may not have been the most reliable defender in the world but, like Serge Blanco, he was capable of moments of genius and, as an attacker, few could match him when he lined out for either Scotland or the Lions. In 1974, the Lions brought Irvine beside J.P.R. Williams on the wing. Although he was out of his position (full-back), he was too good a player to leave on the bench. In full flight, he was guaranteed to quicken the pulse. As a place-kicker, he could be a little erratic. After he missed an easy penalty against England, one of his colleagues told him in no uncertain terms, 'I could have kicked a chest o' drawers over frae there.' Ten minutes later he kicked a conversion from an almost impossible angle. The same colleague told him, 'That was the best conversion since St Paul's.'

When Andy was good he was brilliant, but on a bad day his place-kicking could be badly off. Bill McLaren said of one of his botched penalties, 'That one was a bit inebriated, just like one of my golf shots.'

McLaren also had a comment on one of Irvine's successors as full-back and place-kicker, Peter Dods. His description of the habitual tip-toe dance performed by Dods at the start of each goal-kick run-up was 'Tweet, tweet, tweet'.

### Seeing stars

Like Andy Irvine, the late, great Gordon Brown, 'Broon frae Troon', was one of the legends of rugby. He remains one of Scotland's most famous forwards. He made his debut in Scotland's 6–3 defeat of the Springboks in 1969. In their next match, Scotland lost to France at Murrayfield and he was dropped for the next match against Wales. He heard the news in unusual circumstances. He was working in the bank when he was told there was someone on the phone who had something to do with rugby. Gordon rushed to the phone to discover that the person on the line was his brother Peter, who shouted down the line: 'Great news – I'm back in the Scottish team!'

'Fantastic!' Gordon shouted. 'Who's out?'

Peter replied, 'You are.'

Gordon was distressed by the effects of the pressure to win on young players and on stars in sport in general, specifically referring to a story that some rugby players were reacting to the pressure by taking cocaine. He claimed it gave a whole new meaning to 'powder your nose'.

## Flower of Scotland

He enjoyed hearing strange comments on other sports. Two of his favourites were those of former jockey, Willie Carson – 'I'm lucky because I have an athlete between my legs' – and Bill Cosby – 'The serve was invented in tennis so that the net could play.' However, his all-time favourite was Harry Carpenter's remark at the 1977 Boat Race: 'Ah, isn't that nice, the wife of the Cambridge president is kissing the cox of the Oxford crew.'

When one of the Scottish squad was having problems with his love life, Gordon said: 'The last time he was in a woman was when he went to America and visited the Statue of Liberty.'

In 1981, Ireland lost all of its matches in the Five Nations. In a magazine interview that year, Gordon was asked what made him laugh. He replied, 'Cartoons, Woody Allen and the Irish defence!'

Gordon was not always impressed by the facilities when he went on tour with Scotland. He is remembered for his conversation with a hotel manager. 'I said to the manager, "This is supposed to be a five-star hotel and there's a bloody

Star struck

73

hole in the roof." He turned around and said, "That's where you can see the five stars from.'"

Another famous line was when he was asked about a club game he had played on a frozen pitch. 'As you know, I don't usually complain about pitches but this one was so slippery we had a job to turn around at half-time.' Another time he remarked that the pitch was as level as a billiard ball.

## The Lord's name
In rugby folklore, stories abound about travelling to matches. Gordon Brown often told a story about the Scottish team's visit to Ireland one year. When the team got off the plane and onto the bus at Dublin airport, the elderly bus driver told them what an honour it was to drive them around the city. However, his tune changed dramatically when a policeman boarded the bus and told him, 'Whatever happens, you must follow us and don't stop for anything until we get to the Shelbourne Hotel.'

The blood immediately drained from the driver's face and he said, 'Be Jaysus!'

The bus, with two outriders on motorcycles in front, departed without incident and at a relaxed pace. However, as it got nearer the city centre the speed increased dramatically, running every red light in sight; each time the driver shouted, 'Be Jaysus!' They entered O'Connell Street, where four lanes were going one way and four were going the other. The bus was confronted by four blocked lanes. To the horror of the driver, the outriders bumped across the central reservation, waving him to follow suit. Shouting hysterically, 'Be Jaysus, Be Jaysus!', he bounced the bus across the reservation and headed down O'Connell Street against four lanes of oncoming traffic. The driver put one hand over his eyes and cursed loudly. To his astonishment, one of the outriders stood up on his bike and parted the oncoming cars in the manner of Moses at the Red Sea.

Forty more 'Be Jaysus's later, the bus got out of O'Connell

Street but as it turned left the bus knocked down one of the outriders. With a speed of foot which was exceptional for a man of his age, the bus driver rushed out to help him and as he was saying 'Be Jay–' the other outrider screamed at him to start driving quickly.

Finally, and after a further litany of oaths, the bus reached the hotel. Leaping out of the bus the driver hauled the outrider off his bike and roared: 'Be Jaysus! What was that all about?'

The policeman answered, 'Oh, we were a bit concerned about the team's security. We had a warning from the IRA.'

The driver said, to the surprise of nobody on the bus, 'Be Jaysus!'

The team brought him inside to buy him a drink but on the way in he was searched thoroughly by an armed security guard. All he could say was 'Be Jaysus!' Before he touched the pint of Guinness put before him he asked the Scots when they would be coming back again. When he was told it would be two years, his face seemed to come alive and he drank his pint in one go. He smiled broadly as he put the empty glass on the table. Then he said with a twinkle in his eye: 'Thanks be to Jaysus. I'll be retired by then.'

## Mighty Mouse

Bill Lothian, rugby correspondent with the *Edinburgh Evening News*, once stated that 'The front row is an immensely technical place where brain and brawn collide; it is one which has fascinated me since I played with a prop whose shorts caught fire during a game as a consequence of carrying a light for his half-time fag.' One of Bill's great heroes was 'Mighty Mouse' Ian McLauchlan. The diminutive McLauchlan was capped as a loose-head prop 43 times and captained Scotland in 19 major internationals. There is a famous picture of Ian, on tour with the Lions in 1974, lifting a huge South African prop clean off the ground in a scrummage. His attitude to the game was probably most starkly revealed after he retired, when he was acting as summariser for BBC television. Scotland were playing Ireland at Murrayfield. The Irish lock Neil Francis swung a punch but missed his intended target. Ian was concerned, but not about the violence. With millions of viewers watching, he warned Francis that he was in serious danger of getting the name of a softie because 'there isn't much point in having a go at somebody unless you make sure that you connect'.

Francis waited until 2003 to exact retribution when he struck a damning blow at one of Scotland's most cherished institutions: 'Scotsmen wear kilts because sheep can hear zippers a mile away.'

Mighty Mouse was not always receptive to referees who made bad decisions which cost Scotland. When one disallowed a try which the Scots felt was legitimate, Ian was asked for his verdict afterwards. 'Far be it for me to criticise the referee but I saw him after the match and he was heading straight to the optician's. Guess who he bumped into on the way? Everyone.'

After another referee 'robbed' Scotland of a certain victory, Ian came up with a variation on the theme: 'I was glad to see when the referee went to the shops afterwards he went straight into the optician's. The only problem was that he asked for a packet of cigarettes and a bar of chocolate.'

Mighty Mouse was at the centre of a revealing incident on the 1974 Lions tour. He asked Stewart McKinney which was the greater honour, to play for Ireland or the Lions. Stewart thought for ten seconds before saying Ireland. Ian slapped him on the face. 'Did I say the wrong thing?' asked McKinney.

'No, you gave the right answer.'

'Then why did you slap me?'

'Because it took you ten seconds to find it,' replied McLauchlan.

Today forwards go in for fancy handling but in the old days a forward's job was to get the ball and give it straight to the backs. That is why Mighty Mouse was terrified when someone passed to him in an international at Twickenham. 'Christ, there I was, in the middle of Twickenham with 60,000 looking on, and with this blasted thing in my hands, not knowing what to do with it.'

In 1971, Scotland played England twice on consecutive Saturdays. In the first game, at Twickenham, the tactics in the front row were very 'robust'. One of the England forwards complained bitterly to McLauchlan, 'We don't play like that down here.'

Mighty Mouse retorted, 'Well, sonny boy, you've got a week to find out just how to do it.'

## For medicinal purposes

As in most countries, drink figures prominently in the lore of Scottish rugby. A representative XV from the Border clubs was playing a touring English team. After a clash of heads between the two rival props, the doctor was called as one of the players was temporarily unconscious. As he came round, the doctor said, 'Take him into the changing-room and give him a few drams of malt whisky.'

A voice piped up, 'I think he's a teetotaller.'

The doctor shook his head and said, 'In that case he wouldnae be worth saving.'

A highly respected Scotland international turned up on a chat show on Canadian television totally drunk. The presenter was very unimpressed and asked him why he was so drunk. The Scot replied, 'Well, a few weeks ago I was sitting in a pub in Glasgow and I saw a sign on a beer mat which said "Drink Canada Dry". So when I came over here I said I'd give it a go!'

## It's the way he tells them

In the late '80s, Willie Anderson was chosen as captain of Ireland. The flip-side of the coin was that he had to make the speeches at the dinners. A lot of drink is consumed on those occasions and not everyone wants to listen to a speech. One of his earliest dinners as captain was after a game against Scotland. During his address, he looked down and he could see Kenny Milne with his hand over his mouth trying to hold back the vomit. He could only hope it was from drink and not from listening to his speech.

Willie seemed to have an effect on Scottish players. At another Scottish dinner he was sitting beside Craig Chalmers all night. At the end of the evening, Chalmers had to be carried away on one of the tables.

Willie cannot be held responsible for all the accidents at Scottish dinners. In 1986, the table on which the Scottish tight-head prop Iain 'the Bear' Milne was leaning at the post-match dinner in Cardiff collapsed. Milne's response was to say, 'Waiter, bring me another table.'

As a forward, Milne did not enjoy the expansive game. In 1988, he was asked if he was happy that the pitch was just right for fast, open, running rugby. Milne's reply was, 'The conditions are bloody awful.'

## All I need is the air that I breathe

Scottish referees, like their goalkeepers, sometimes get a bad press. A Scottish referee who will remain nameless was making his international debut at Twickenham in an England–Ireland Five Nations fixture in the 1970s. Willie Duggan was having a fag in the Irish dressing-room. The time had come to run on to the pitch but Duggan had nowhere to put out his cigarette. He knew that if he ran out in the tunnel with the fag in his mouth the cameras would zoom in on him straight away. When the referee came in to tell the teams it was time to leave, the Irish number 8 went over to him and said, 'Would you hold that for a second please?' The obliging referee said yes and Duggan promptly ran out onto the pitch – leaving the ref with no option but to put out the fag. He went out to face the glare of the cameras and the first sight the television audience had of him he was holding a cigarette! Asked about the incident afterwards the referee said, 'I've had a wonderful day – but this wasn't it.'

The referee did have the last word, though, at the post-match dinner when Duggan asked him if he minded his smoking. He said, 'I don't mind your smoking if you don't mind my being sick all over you.'

## The Tower of Babel

Language barriers can be a serious problem in exhibition games. In the 1970s, an all-star cast was assembled to play a club team. The celebrity team included Gareth Edwards, Gerald Davies and the Scot Ian Barnes. Barnes was a second-row forward from the Borders, who speaks with a thick Scottish accent. His scrummaging partner was Moss Keane, who speaks with a thick Irish accent. They were sorting out tactics before the match but were incapable of communicating through words. By using gestures and amid vigorous nodding of their heads they seemed to have worked something out. On the pitch, however, the scrum was a total disaster. The touring side were losing by 20 points at half-time. Barnes went to Edwards and said, 'Hey, Gareth, I cannae understand what he's saying. I'm pushing on the wrong side of the scrum. Would you think you could get him to swap sides with me?'

A minute later Keane went up to Edwards and said, 'That bloody Scot can't speak f**king English. I'm pushing on the wrong side.' Edwards brokered a compromise and the tourists were a transformed side in the second half and won the match.

## Rallying cry

In 1925 John Bannerman was the captain of Scotland's Grand Slam-winning side.

Everybody knew his bike. He never locked it because no one would dare touch it. Once he was speaking to an ever increasing circle of rugby fans about a big match when he held his bicycle in the air. When asked by an onlooker what he was doing, he replied, 'I'm holding a Raleigh!'

## Time, gentlemen, please

Herbert Waddell was an outstanding fly-half for Glasgow Academicals and Scotland, and gained rugby legend status through the drop-goal, then worth four points, that won the Grand Slam for Scotland in the 14–11 defeat of England at Murrayfield in 1925.

In the build-up to an international against England, Herbert went to bed early the night before the first training session. Training was scheduled for 9.30 the next morning but when he woke up the next day and looked at his watch it was 11.30. Herbert panicked and ran down the corridor to reception, dressing as he ran. When he got to reception, he was out of breath and asked the porter, 'Can you please phone me a taxi? I'm late for training.'

The porter replied, 'Are you crazy? It's only 6.20 in the morning.'

Herbert's watch had stopped at 11.30 p.m. the previous night.

Years later a friend told him that he was setting up a watch repair shop. Herbert suggested a slogan for him: 'Come in and see us when you don't have the time.'

Herbert had a reputation for speaking bluntly. One story told about him is that when he went to visit a sick friend in hospital he brought him in some magazines, but when he saw how sick he looked he said, 'If I were you, I wouldn't bother starting any serials.'

## Snakes and ladders

Rugby fortunes are a fickle thing. In 1984, Scotland were on a high having won the Grand Slam. A few months later, they were well beaten by Australia. Asked to comment on the reversal of Scottish fortunes Aussie coach Alan Jones said, 'One day you're a rooster, the next a feather duster.'

# Flower of Scotland

No one knows the slings and arrows of outrageous rugby fortune better than Scottish fans. They have known the lows, including a 44–0 trouncing by the Springboks at Murrayfield in 1951 that held the record for an international defeat until Romania lost to Ireland 60–0 at Lansdowne Road in 1986. But there have been highs, too, notably when they sensationally defeated hot favourites England to claim the Grand Slam 13–7 at Murrayfield on Saint Patrick's Day, 17 March 1990. In the final moments, with victory in sight, one extremely voluble Scottish fan in the East Stand broke the habit of a lifetime and offered a wine gum to the English woman beside him. She replied, 'Can I have two, please? One for each ear.'

## War without bullets

It's not that Scottish rugby fans hate the English but . . .

One incident that sums up Scottish fans' feelings for English rugby happened after Jonny Wilkinson played his first match at Murrayfield. The English squad walked past John Rutherford, who was talking to a sweet elderly lady. John turned around to Wilkinson and said, 'Congratulations, Jonny.'

After exchanging a few words, the English out-half ran on to catch up with the squad. He was almost out of earshot when he heard John saying to the woman: 'That's Jonny Wilkinson, the England player.'

Her reply to this information was, 'I know. I hate him!'

Two other stories illustrate the 'mutual affection' between the two rugby nations. At Christmas 1990, after Scotland had won the Grand Slam, an English family went into Manchester to do some Christmas shopping. In the sports shop, the son picked up a Scotland rugby shirt and said to his twin sister, 'I've decided to be a Scotland supporter and I would like this jersey for Christmas.'

His sister, outraged by the suggestion, slapped him on the face and said, 'Go talk to your mother.'

The boy walked with the Scotland shirt in hand and found his mother. 'Mummy dearest?'

'Yes, pet?'

'I've decided I'm going to be a Scotland supporter and I'd like this shirt for Christmas.'

The mother could barely speak with anger but eventually said, 'Go talk to your father.'

Off he went with shirt in hand and found his father. 'Dad?'

'Yes, son?'

'I've decided to become a Scotland supporter and I would like this shirt for Christmas.'

The father hit the son a thump on the head and said, 'No son of mine will be seen in a thing like that.'

As they went home the father asked the son if he had learned any lesson that day. The son thought for a moment before replying, 'Yes, I have. I've only been a Scotland fan for about an hour and already I hate you English f\*\*kers!'

Another story is of the England fan based in Glasgow who got so depressed after Scotland beat England in 1990 that he dressed up in his full England kit and threw himself in the river. When the Scottish police retrieved his body, they removed the strip and replaced it with stockings and suspenders. They told the coroner that they did this 'in order to avoid embarrassing the family'.

English fans are well able to get their own back. One story they tell is of the doctor who encouraged his patient to start watching Scotland. The doctor said he should avoid any excitement.

They also revel in the unfortunate stereotypical image of Scottish people as mean, revealed in stories like the one about the Scottish rugby international who gave his wife lipstick for Christmas every year so that at least he could get half of it back.

Another story they tell in this context is about the Pope. He had a very, very unusual blood type. He was ill and needed a transfusion but the doctors could only find one person in the whole world who had the same type: Jimmy Burns from Scotland. So Jimmy donated a pint of blood and the Pope recovered. As a gesture of goodwill the Pope sent Jimmy £20,000. The Pope got ill four times in successive years after that and each time he got a pint of Jimmy's blood and each time he sent Jimmy £20,000. The sixth time he got Jimmy's blood the Pope sent him only a holy medal. Jimmy was devastated and rang the Vatican to ask why he'd got no money this time. The Pope's secretary took the call and answered, 'Well, Jimmy, you have to understand he has a lot of Scots blood in him at this stage.'

The English fans also claim that whenever the Scottish team go on a tour, any hotel they stay in puts its Gideon Bibles on chains.

After Scotland's particularly disappointing Six Nations campaign in 2004, the level of English ridicule went into overdrive. One of their stories was about a hole in the wall outside Murrayfield which allowed some of the Scottish fans to sneak into the game for free. The ground manager put an extra security man on duty at the hole in the wall. During the game against England, 50 people tried to access the spot at the one time. The security guard was furious. He roared at them, 'How unpatriotic of you to leave the game when there's still 20 minutes to go. Get back in there. I'm not letting you out till the game is over. Why should you lot not suffer like everyone else?'

The English fans were particularly scornful of the Scottish backs. One was heard to remark, 'They're so lethargic they would get blisters pointing.'

Scottish clubs have failed to match sides like Bath or Leicester on the European stage. After Edinburgh's loss in France in the Heineken Cup quarter-final in April 2004, one English wag asked and answered the question: 'What's the similarity between a three-point plug and Edinburgh? – They're both bloody useless in Europe.'

Even when their rugby fortunes are at a low, the Scots always get the last word. They tell the story of three Scotsmen and three Englishmen travelling by train to a match at

Murrayfield. At the station, the three Englishmen each buy a ticket and watch as the three Scotsmen only buy a single ticket between the three of them. 'How are the three of you going to travel on the train?' asks one of the English.

'Watch and learn,' replies one of the Scots.

They all board the train. The English take their seats but all three Scots cram into a toilet and close the door behind them. Shortly after the train departs, the conductor arrives to collect the tickets. He knocks on the toilet door and says, 'Ticket, please.' The door opens just a crack and a single arm emerges with a ticket in hand. The conductor takes it and moves on. The Englishmen are very impressed, so after the match they decide to imitate their Scottish brethren on the way home. When they get to the station, they buy a single ticket for the journey. To their amazement, the Scots buy not even a single ticket. 'How are the three of you going to travel on the train?' asks one of the English.

'Watch and learn,' replies one of the Scots.

Once they board, the three Englishmen lock themselves in one toilet and the three Scots lock themselves in another one nearby. The train departs. A short while afterwards, one of the Scots leaves the toilet, knocks on the toilet door where the English are locked in and says, 'Ticket, please . . .'

## Money, money, money

A Scotsman turned up at a rugby match with his wife and eleven children. He presented two tickets at the turnstile and started to usher his family through. 'Just a minute,' said the attendant, 'where are the other tickets?'

'Your advertisement said children under 12 admitted free. So count them! There's only 11 here, we left the youngest at home. Isn't that under 12?'

Scottish administrators have a reputation for a Scrooge-like mentality when it comes to ensuring that every penny is spared. Harry Simpson, SRU secretary, always boosted a player's confidence; he habitually attached a handwritten note to a player's notice of selection which read as follows: 'If you are not selected for the following match, you're instructed to return your jersey.'

In the 1920s, professionalism was not even dreamed of. When Jimmy Ireland went to his boss at the Singer Manufacturing Company in Glasgow to request a Saturday off to play for Scotland his boss replied, 'Do you really need the whole day?'

## Rugby spirits in the sky

During a Calcutta Cup match, there was a lightning strike and both Clive Woodward and Ian McGeechan were sadly killed. They both ascended to heaven and, given their status in the rugby hierarchy, they bypassed St Peter at the pearly gates and were brought in the VIP entrance where they were greeted by no less than God himself. 'Greetings. Heaven is enriched by having both of you here. Come on, I'll show your accommodation. I hope you'll both be comfortable.'

God took Clive by the hand and led him off on a short walk through beautiful fields of flowers until they came across a pretty thatched cottage by a stream, with a beautiful garden, lovely flower beds and tall trees swaying in the gentle breeze. The thatched roof formed the shape of St George's Cross, the birds in the trees were whistling 'Swing Low, Sweet Chariot' and the gnomes by the garden path were images of great English rugby heroes: David Duckham, Rory Underwood, Fran Cotton and Bill Beaumont.

Woodward was left uncharacteristically speechless. Eventually he muttered, 'I don't know what to say.'

God then took McGeechan up the path. As they were strolling away, Clive looked around him and, further up the road, he saw a gigantic mansion, with massive pillars carved like thistles, Scottish lions rampant on the gates and fields of heather all around. The house and gardens were surrounded by stands of Scots pine and Douglas fir. On the manicured lawns, there were huge 20-foot golden statues of John Rutherford, Roy Laidlaw, Craig Chalmers, Finlay Calder and the two Hastings brothers overlooking a beautiful, magnificent garden. Massed choirs of birds were singing 'Flower of Scotland' in harmonies that the Everly Brothers would have marvelled at. A little flustered, Clive ran after God and his old rival and, tapping God on the shoulder, said, 'Excuse me, God, I don't wish to sound ungrateful or anything, but I was wondering why Ian's house is so much more stylish than mine.'

God smiled beatifically at him and said: 'There, there, Clive, don't worry, it's not Ian's house. It's mine!'

# THREE

# Welsh Wit

### Gareth the Barbarian

> This is great stuff. Phil Bennett covering, chased by
> Alistair Scown. Brilliant! Oh, that's brilliant! John
> Williams . . . Pullin . . . John Dawes. Great dummy.
> David, Tom David; the halfway line. Brilliant by
> Quinnell. This is Gareth Edwards. A dramatic start.
> WHAT A SCORE!

Cliff Morgan's commentary on the most talked about try in one
of the most talked about games of all time, when the Barbarians
beat New Zealand 23–11 on 27 January 1973. That score is
now universally known as 'that try' in the same way as
Elizabeth Hurley's revealing outfit for the premiere of *Four*

*Weddings and a Funeral* is known simply as 'that dress'. It is right and fitting that it was scored by the Welsh wizard, Gareth Edwards. He may not have been as beautiful as Elizabeth Hurley, but nobody has ever made a more determined attempt to make rugby the beautiful game. It was also appropriate that it was Edwards who was chosen as the player of the last millennium by a leading rugby magazine. Asked to comment on that selection, Willie John McBride said, 'When I get to the pearly gates and they say, "What are your qualifications for coming in here?" I'll say I knew Gareth Edwards.'

Such was Gareth's impact that when he played in an Under-nines match, with the team leading by 30–6 at half-time, the coach told him to give the opposition a chance and pass the ball more. The young Edwards answered: 'Ah, coach, you're only wasting your time. If I pass it they'll just knock it on or drop it.'

Welsh players are proud of their ex-internationals on and off the field. It was reported to Gareth Edwards that a retired international had been caught with a call-girl early one winter's morning in a park.

'Now,' said Edwards, 'let's get this straight. Are you saying he was actually with a young girl at 6 o'clock in the morning, with frost on the grass? And he was 75?' The report was confirmed as correct.

'By God!' chortled Gareth. 'Makes one proud to be Welsh.'

Gareth is a big angling fan. He once said he would rather reel in a big salmon after a good fight than score a try for Wales. He described his biggest catch: 'It was fully 17 lb. It was bigger than Barry John.'

Prior to one Murrayfield international, he had a couple of days' fishing on the Tweed at Kelso. There he was, up to his waders and just under the main bridge at Kelso with all his gear when three jolly faces appeared on the bridge all festooned in the red and white of Wales. The Welsh fans were from Gareth's own territory of Cwmgors and gazed down in wonder before asking, 'Hey, Gar, boyo, what you'm doin' down there?'

Ever the gentleman, Gareth resisted the strong temptation to say, 'I'm signing bloody autographs, in' I?'

He regretted his reticence when one of them said, 'Gar, you'd score a lot more tries for Wales if it wasn't for those rusty kneecaps of yours from all that fishing.'

When there was a rumour that he had undergone major heart treatment in hospital, Gareth quipped, 'I've never had major knee surgery on any other part of my body.'

## Call boys

In the mid-'70s, Wales decided on a signal at set scrums to tell the forwards which way the backs intended to move the ball so that the support players knew exactly where to go. The two flankers were Trevor Evans from Swansea and Terry Cobner from Pontypool. It was agreed that any word beginning with 'S' for Swansea would mean the move was going left whereas an initial 'P' would indicate right. Eventually, confident that everybody understood, it was time to take the new ploy onto the practice field and Gareth Edwards was the man to make the call just before he put in the ball. He shouted, 'Psychology!' The Pontypool front row went left, the rest of the forwards went right and the result was chaos.

## Loose men

Gareth Edwards sustained an injury playing against England. In the dressing-room afterwards Barry John asked him what he was going to do. Gareth said he wasn't too bothered because he had just discovered a wonderful female masseuse. Barry asked, 'What's so good about this particular masseuse?'

Edwards innocently replied within earshot of the entire team, 'The beauty of this girl is that she'll drop anything for a rugby player!'

Within weeks the masseuse had an expanded practice of almost 20 Welsh internationals!

## Little and little

A journalist looking for a sensational story after Wales won one of their Triple Crowns asked Gareth Edwards and Phil Bennett if they had thought about defecting to rugby league. When Edwards rejected the idea out of hand, the hack turned to Phil and said, 'Gareth is looking down on rugby league, Phil, how about you?'

'When you're as small as me you can't afford to look down on anything,' Phil replied.

## A hard day's night

Today's rugby players are children of their times, conditioned by rugby's social climate and personifying its prevalent ethos. Efficiency and pragmatism are the virtues they live by. They stand for what is deemed necessary for success in rugby today: hard-headed, tough, no-nonsense realism in place of romanticism and sentimentality. The great Welsh team of the 1970s were cut from a different cloth. They travelled together in groups for squad sessions. On the way home, they had a number of stops for 'light refreshments'. They came home at all hours of the day and night. Phil Bennett's wife could never understand how a training session could last 24 hours!

On one occasion, she gave Phil the evil eye when he returned home hours late. The man with the magic sidestep said, 'Darling, I married you for your looks but not the kind of looks I'm getting now.'

Another joke told about Phil is that when he came home late one night from 'training', his wife had already gone to bed. 'Is my dinner warm?' he bellowed up the stairs.

'Only if the dustbin's on fire,' she yelled back.

## Celtic warriors

As captain of the Lions team that toured New Zealand in 1977, Bennett needed players willing to shed blood for the cause. He found one in Willie Duggan.

## Welsh Wit

During one match, Willie was so battered and bloodied that he went off for stitches just before half-time. When the rest of the team came into the dressing-room they saw him sitting there with a fag in one hand and a bottle of beer in the other as they stitched up his face. 'Bad luck, Willie, well played,' Bennett said.

'What do you mean?' Willie demanded. 'As soon as these f**kers sort my face out I'll be back on.'

On the tour, Willie played for the Lions against a Maori team in a very physical contest. At one stage he was trapped at the bottom of a ruck when a few players kicked him on his head. True to form he got up and carried on. After the game Bennett asked him if he remembered the pounding on his head. His reply was vintage Dugganesque: 'I do. I heard it.'

Phil always enjoyed his trips to Dublin for the social aspect. After the post-match dinner, some of the Irish players were intent on stretching the evening with the Welsh team a bit further and hit a local nightclub. On entering the premises, Moss Keane beckoned to Willie Duggan. 'What'll ye have, Willie?'

Duggan replied, 'Moss, I'll have a creamy pint of stout, from the middle of the barrel.'

Following a brief exchange at the bar, Moss returned and said sadly, 'They've no beer here at all, Willie, only wine.'

'Oh,' replied Duggan, 'I'll have a pint of wine, so.'

Later that night, Bennett said to Gareth Edwards, 'Moss Keane has legs on him like a drinks cabinet.'

Gareth replied, 'That's appropriate, considering the amount he drinks.'

Getting in on the act, Bennett said, 'Moss and Willie read that drink was bad for you. They gave up reading. Throughout their careers they've lived by the adage that "moderate drinkers live longer and it serves them right".'

At a fund-raising dinner for Moldovan orphans during a visit to Dublin in 2003, Phil joked, 'In 1982, as Ireland stood on the threshold of winning the Triple Crown, Moss made the ultimate sacrifice and cut his drink in half. He left out the water. Years later, Moss was persuaded to join Alcoholics Anonymous. Subsequently he has been drinking under an assumed name.'

Phil also recalled another classic story in rugby folklore about Moss from one of his tours with the Barbarians in Wales. At one stage his team went to the bar after a game of golf. Although everybody else was drinking beer, Moss, with commendable patriotism, was drinking Guinness and knocking back two pints to everyone else's one. As dinner time approached, it was decided it was time to return to the team hotel. As people prepared to leave, somebody shouted, 'one for the road'. Ten pints later for the team at large, and twenty pints later for Moss, the team was again summoned to the team bus. Moss was asked if he thought they should stay for one more drink. He shook his head. When questioned as to why he was opposed to the idea Moss replied. 'To be sure, I don't want to be making a pig of myself.'

Bennett also recalled how Moss was once selected to play for the Welsh Barbarians against a touring South Africa team. The game turned violent, with numerous bouts of fisticuffs. At one stage, 29 of the players on the field were fighting. Moss was the sole non-combatant. Asked later why he had been so uncharacteristically Gandhian, Moss replied, 'I might die for Ireland but I'm f**ked if I'm going to die for Wales.'

## Church or Chapel?

In his book *A Patch of Glory*, Alan Richards refers to Welsh out-halfs as being either High Church or Chapel. From this perspective Barry John and Gareth Davies belonged to the High Church while Cliff Morgan and Phil Bennett belonged to the Chapel.

The distinction was that the High Church type of number 10 tended to play without any apparent effort, exerting the minimum amount of energy to the maximum effect, while the other relied much more on physical activity. The theory was that when the intellect ruled the heart there was a more subtle, sophisticated approach. However, the 'busy-busy' type was not necessarily less effective.

A less cerebral use of religious language to talk about the great Welsh players is revealed in the following story:

Welsh fan: Look, there's Barry John.

English fan: So what, he's not the Almighty.

Welsh fan: No, but he's young yet.

Barry was always in great demand to play in exhibition games. His box-office value is illustrated in the story told by Cliff Morgan that there was a large sign outside a rugby ground before a match which read: 'Admission £2. If Barry John Plays – £10.'

Although his nickname was 'the King', the Welsh management were able to ensure that Barry never got too big for his boots. When John Dawes retired from the Welsh captaincy, Barry's name was widely linked with the post. One headline writer proclaimed, 'This is the Crowning of the True King'. Barry did not want the extra responsibilities of captaincy and he telephoned the Welsh manager, Clive Rowlands, to air his concerns. Rowlands took the wind out of his sails by saying, 'Don't worry, we haven't even considered you, Barry.'

Another wag was heard to remark after an uncharacteristic off-day, 'Barry John can make the ball talk. The problem is it's saying goodbye.'

## J.P.R.

It was Mae West who famously said, 'A hard man is good to find.' In the 1970s, Welsh fans had the same comment to make about J.P.R. Williams. He did not take any prisoners with his tough tackling. Hence a Welsh fan's banner at Murrayfield: 'A haggis a day doesn't keep Dr J.P.R. away'.

It is interesting to contrast his attitude to full-back play with that of the other great full-back of the second half of the twentieth century, Serge Blanco. Serge had a more sensual, 'French' attitude to the game: 'Rugby is just like love. You have to give before you can take. And when you have the ball it's like making love – you must think of the other's pleasure before your own.' Yet when J.P.R. struck the line it was devastating.

Rugby players have tongues as sharp as cactii. J.P.R. played as a flanker in an international against Australia in 1978. His versatility was such that some of his teammates helpfully suggested that the night the tour party returned home to Wales, traditionally a night of passion as the players intimately reacquainted themselves with their significant others, they should send a telegram to J.P.R.'s other half saying, 'We've tried J.P.R. out in 15 different positions but with limited success. We hope you'll have more luck tonight.'

J.P.R. was good at giving advice himself. A young man once said to him: 'I've half a mind to become a rugby player.'

J.P.R. replied, 'That's all you need.'

## The battle of the bulge
Bobby Windsor, 'the Duke', was the hooker on the great Welsh team of the '70s and is one of the most celebrated individuals of them all in rugby folklore. He once joked that the epitaph for many ex-players who have lost the battle of the bulge could be the same as that of Paddy Drury:

> Here lie the bones of Paddy Drury,
> Owing their size to the local brewery.

When one of his colleagues who was coming to the end of his career started to put on a lot of weight, Bobby joked that he was 'finally pulling his weight in the Welsh jersey'.

## The Pontypool Three
Great prop forwards like France's Robert Paparemborde,

'Papa', have always graced the game. However, any discussion of the great front rows must begin with the Wales and Pontypool front row of Charlie Faulkner, Bobby Windsor and Graham Price, famed in song and story, especially the famous 'The Ballad of the Pontypool Front Row' by Max Boyce:

> There's a programme on the telly,
> I see it when I can,
> The story of an astronaut,
> The first bionic man.
> He cost 6 million dollars,
> That's a lot of bread I know,
> But Wigan offered more than that
> For the Pontypool front row.

The camaraderie between front-row players is amazing, especially with the Pontypool gang, who first played together for Wales against France in 1975 and went on to play 18 further games in the Welsh front row. It is a strange fact of rugby life that people in positions close to each other on the field tend to pal around together. Their motto was: 'We may go up and we may go down, but we *never* go back.'

It was said that Windsor's tactic with novice opponents was to bite them on the ear early in the match and say, 'Behave yourself, son, and nothing will happen to this ear of yours.'

Faulkner tells the story that when Wales travelled to play England at Twickenham in the '70s, Graham Price was walking through London when he saw a man lying dead on the street. He raced to the nearest phone box and rang the police. He told the cop the situation and the boy in blue replied, 'OK, you're there in Tottenham Court Road. Spell Tottenham Court Road.'

Graham started, 'T-O-T . . . no, T-O-T-T . . . no.' He paused and said, 'Hang on a few minutes. I'm just going to drag him round to Oxford Street and I'll ring you back then.'

Bobby Windsor once told a story about his partner in the front row, Charlie Faulkner. In 1980, some of the Welsh guys played in a tournament match in France. The match was played in mid-July. In the middle of the summer, Charlie was totally unfit. The game passed right by him. At one stage, Windsor saw him stamping on the ground. He went over to him and asked him what the hell he was doing. Faulkner answered, 'Oh, I'm stamping that bloody snail which has been following me around since the match started.'

Snail's pace

In retaliation, Faulkner told a story about Windsor. In the late 1970s, the two lined out together on a celebrity team in an exhibition match against a Welsh club side to mark the club's centenary. The celebrity team were badly beaten. Nobody said much in the visitors' dressing-room afterwards because they were so disappointed with their performance. At the back of the stand, Windsor met two guys with their arms around each other. One of them recognised the great Welsh hooker and said, 'I know this is our centenary year, but there's no need to play like one of the founding members!'

## Eggs-actly

Bobby had some great exchanges with waiters during the '74 Lions tour. One went as follows:

Windsor: I want one egg boiled for exactly 26 seconds and I want another one boiled for 25 minutes 14 seconds. And I want three slices of toast which are pale gold on one side and burned pure black on the other.

Waiter: But, sir, that's simply not possible. We can't go to all that trouble to fill one order.

Windsor: Oh yes you can, sonny boy. That's exactly what you dished up to me yesterday.

At another meal, the players were tucking into a big steak dinner. Bobby was feeling a bit under the weather and just asked for an omelette. The waiter asked, 'What kind of omelette would you like, sir?' Bobby just looked up at him and barked, 'A f**king egg omelette!'

When one waiter was getting hopelessly lost as he took orders from a hungry Lions squad, Windsor instructed him to do a bit of mental arithmetic with a calculator.

Windsor was one of the game's great raconteurs. One of his favourite stories was about a Welsh Valleys rugby club on tour in America. On coming back from a night on the town, two of the players could not find their rooms. They decided to check for their teammates by looking through the keyholes. At one stage they came upon an astonishing sight. There in her birthday suit was a Marilyn Monroe lookalike. Close by was a man who was chanting out with great conviction, 'Your face is so beautiful that I will have it painted in gold. Your breasts are so magnificent that

I will have them painted in silver. Your legs are so shapely that I will have them painted in platinum.' Outside, the two Welshmen were getting very aroused and began jostling each other for the right to the keyhole. The man inside, hearing the racket, shouted out, 'Who the hell is out there?'

The two Welsh men replied, 'We're two painters from Pontypool.'

On the Lions' flight to South Africa in 1974, Windsor was taken ill with food poisoning. He was so ill that he was taken to the back of the plane and told to suck ice cubes to help him cool down. The team doctor, former Irish international Ken Kennedy, came to take his temperature without knowing about the ice cubes. When he looked at the thermometer, he shouted out, 'Jaysus, Bobby, you died 24 hours ago!'

During the golden age of amateurism, the manager of the 1974 Lions tour was Alan Thomas. He tended to lose things, especially room keys. He had a phone in his room but each player on the team was only allowed one phone call a week. Bobby Windsor spotted Alan's key and held on to it. Every evening he used it to sneak into Alan's room and phone his wife. As the tour concluded and the team were leaving the hotel, Alan came into the foyer and addressed the entire squad in a crestfallen voice. 'I'm very disappointed. I have been handed a phone bill for a thousand rand. One of you guys has been using the phone every night behind my back. The Lions are supposed to be the cream of rugby but one of you has let the side down in this way. Sadly the guy who did this is a countryman of my own. He's been ringing Pontypridd.'

At this point, Bobby Windsor jumped up from his seat and started waving his fists menacingly as he said, 'Which of you b*****ds has been phoning my wife?'

### Soft centres
One of the great Welsh team of the 1970s, Ray Gravell, was celebrated for his tough tackling. Hence the banner that

appeared at Cardiff Arms Park: 'Ray Gravell Eats Soft Centres'.

Ray relished the physical side of rugby, although he had a curious way of describing it: 'I like to get in one really good tackle early in the game, even if it is late.'

Ray, like a lot of the Welsh players, is very nationalistic. Once, before an international with Ireland, when Mick Quinn was an Irish sub, he went into the toilet and he heard Ray in the next cubicle singing arias about the welcome in the hills in Wales. Quinn told him that the only reason they welcomed people in the hills was that they were too mean to invite them into their homes.

There was a limit to the amount of Ray's singing Quinn could take so he asked him to give it a rest but he went on and on. To shut him up Quinn filled a bucket of cold water, threw it over Ray in the cubicle and fled. When the Welsh team came out, some of the Irish players remarked that Ray must have gone through an awfully heavy warm-up because the sweat was rolling off him.

During that match, Ray heard the instructions from the Irish forwards during a mêlée after a ruck: 'Kick ahead, Ireland, kick ahead. Any bloody head.' Maybe that's why Richard Burton defined rugby as 'ballet, opera and sheer bloody murder'.

Ray offers a bizarre illustration of the importance of self-confidence to a player. He consistently required reassurance on the field about his performance. This was used against him by some of his international colleagues when they met in club matches. A typical ploy was to approach him early in a match and ask him if he was feeling OK. Gravell would be thrown into a panic straight away and enquire what prompted the question. He would be told in a most concerned voice that although he looked the picture of health the previous week when he played so well for Wales, now he looked very sickly indeed. As a result, his confidence would go to pieces and he would be totally ineffective until some of his Llanelli teammates reassured him he was in the prime of health.

An incident which revealed his insecurity occurred on the 1980 Lions tour when he was sharing a room with John O'Driscoll. One morning O'Driscoll said with a flourish, 'I slept really well.'

Gravell's response was made in tones of hushed anxiety. 'I slept all right, too, didn't I?'

Gravell also had a mischievous streak. The only unpardonable sin on a Lions tour is to miss training. No matter how awful you feel or how low your morale is, you simply must get out to the training field at the appointed hour. Sunday was a day for total relaxation. To pass the afternoon, Gravell and O'Driscoll played a card game with a difference. The penalty if you lost a hand was to take a drink – a mixture of spirits and orange juice. When John lost, he noticed, Ray was adding extra spirits to his drink. John thought he was being very clever by saying nothing and adding a lot of extra juice. What he didn't know was that Gravell had laced the orange juice with large amounts of spirits. The next morning O'Driscoll had the mother of all hangovers and had to miss training.

## Conflict of perceptions

Any discussion of the greatest wingers of all time will very quickly turn to the peerless Gerald Davies. He was so fast that when he was going to bed he could switch off the electric light and be under the sheets before the room went dark.

Gerald once scored a controversial try against Scotland. Bill McLaren told him afterwards that the try should not have been allowed; Gerald replied, James Bond-style, 'Oh, actually that wasn't my impression.'

Davies had huge admiration for J.P.R. Williams, but he once told a story to poke fun at his heroic status. Gerald recalled his first match on the wing in the high-pressure zone at Stade Colombes in Paris. To soothe his frayed nerves he sought consolation from an old hand. J.P.R. spent a lot of time talking with the wingers before the match. The froth was coming out of his mouth, he was so fired up. He warned Davies and his partner on the wing about the way the French would bombard them with high balls. The consoling thing, though, was that he assured them he would be there beside them to take the pressure off them. The match was barely on when the French out-half kicked this almighty ball up in the air between Williams and Davies. To Gerald's horror he heard J.P.R. shouting, 'Your ball!' So much for all that brothers-in-arms talk. Davies caught the ball and nearly got killed as half the French team jumped on top of him.

Wales won four successive Triple Crowns from 1976 to 1979. The downside was that this great team were allowed to grow old together when they should have been gradually replaced by new talent. There were a lot of jokes about the Welsh team as 'Dad's army' because they were getting to be so old. In fact, it was said to be harder to get off the Welsh forward line than it was to get on it.

## Magic Merv

Among the stars of that team was Mervyn Davies. 'Merv the Swerve' was a tough man and didn't mind everybody knowing it. After he was involved in a little 'softening up' of his opposite number, his opponent said, 'You're a dirty b*****d, Davies,' literally taking it on the chin.

'Yeah,' said Merv, 'and don't you forget it.' As if to prove the point, he caught him again late in the second half with a tackle that was so late he must have launched it in the first half.

## Nostalgia's not what it used to be

After the great successes of the 1970s, Wales went through an incredible slump in the late '80s and early '90s before recapturing former glories with a stylish Grand Slam win in 2005. A revealing indicator of how the mighty had fallen was

Gareth Davies' observation, 'We've lost seven of our last eight matches. The only team we beat was Western Samoa. Good job we didn't play the whole of Samoa.' In the 1991 World Cup, however, Wales sensationally lost 16–13 to Western Samoa.

In 1991, when Welsh centre Mark Ring captained the Barbarians to a 46–34 win over the East Midlands, he said when asked about the experience, 'It's lovely to get a break from losing international matches.'

To show that the spirit of flair in Welsh rugby was not fully extinguished, Ring went for a dramatic conclusion to the match. He unsuccessfully attempted to back-heel the final conversion.

The fall in Welsh fortunes in the late '80s is reflected in the following story. Two bricklayers were chatting at work. 'Are you going to the match on Sunday?' said one. 'Wales are playing England.'

'No,' said the other, 'my wife won't let me.'

'What?' said the first. 'It's easy to get out of that. About an hour before the game, what you do is pick her up, take her to the bedroom, rip off her clothes and make mad passionate love to her. Then she'll let you do anything you want.'

'I'll try that,' said the other man.

The following Monday the two men met on the building site. 'How come you didn't make it to the game?' asked the first man.

'Well, I'll tell you what happened,' said the second man. 'About an hour before I was planning to leave, I did as you said. I picked her up, took her to the bedroom and ripped off her clothes, and then I thought, Wales haven't been playing that well lately.'

Wales's place in the rugby hierarchy in 2004 was most manifest in their defeat to the English in the Six Nations. Afterwards an old joke was recycled:

Q: What is the difference between Cinderella and the Welsh side?

A: At least Cinderella got to the ball.

# Welsh Wit

## Holmes and away

Terry Holmes had the almost impossible task of succeeding Gareth Edwards as Welsh scrum-half. A young autograph hunter was chuffed to bits when he got Terry's autograph after a match. The following week he accosted Terry again for his autograph, and after the very next game he tried to get it again.

'Look,' said Terry, 'this is the third time you've asked me for my autograph. What's going on?'

'Well,' said the youngster, 'if I can get eight more of yours, I can swap them for one of Gareth Edwards'.'

Holmes was very tall and in another era, like Danie Gerber, he would probably be picked as a forward in schools rugby because of his upper-body strength. Before Wales played England at Twickenham he predicted the outcome of the particular match in the best tradition of Welsh talkers: 'The first half will be even. The second half will be even harder.'

## Paying the Bill

Every rugby fan loved watching the great Welsh team. However, the only people who seemed to be lukewarm were a tiny but influential minority: the bureaucrats who ruled Welsh rugby at the time. Many administrators had the same attitude as Bill Clement. Bill was secretary of the Welsh Rugby Union during the days when amateurism was adhered to rigidly and with a zeal that even the most fanatical champion of the Spanish Inquisition would have admired. One day, the legendary Welsh hooker Bobby Windsor approached him. Having given sterling service for years to both Wales and the Lions, Bobby decided that the WRU should at least help him with the hire fees for the dinner suit he was obliged to wear at official dinners. So he went to see Bill Clement. Bobby explained how times were hard in the steel industry in Gwent, and, like many others, he had been put on short time. His wife and family were feeling the pinch and every bit of extra cash would help. 'So, if maybe the Union could help me out by hiring the dinner suits, then that would be appreciated,' said Windsor.

'I'm sorry,' replied Clement. 'That's against the rules.'

'Well, what about my shoes?' said Bobby, getting a bit agitated. 'Surely you could help me out and allow me to buy a decent pair of shoes to look smart in? These ones are falling apart.' At this juncture, to emphasise the point, he took off his shoe and showed Clement across the desk how the sole was flapping at the toes. Bill thought about it for a few seconds and then quietly opened a drawer in his desk marked 'Ticket Money'. He took out a huge bundle of notes and untied them from their tightly wound rubber band. As Bobby was waiting for him to count out the cash, Clement chucked the rubber band over to Bobby and said, 'Here, that should sort out the problem with your shoes.'

Another story told about Bill, though its veracity has been challenged, is that when two Welsh internationals were rooming together the night before a game, one went down for a haircut and charged it to their room. Some time later, Bill billed the two lads for half a haircut each!

## Burning bras?

Sometimes rugby officials are caught out when they are unexpectedly thrown into the media spotlight. Before Wales played Scotland in 1962 in Cardiff, the ground was so frozen that the Welsh committee decided on a repeat of their success of 1893, the match with England, when they burned 18 tons of coal during the night to soften the pitch. Not surprisingly the Welsh authorities used braziers to burn the coal. However, when the Welsh Rugby Union president was interviewed on BBC radio to explain the procedure, he said they had used 'dozens of brassieres'.

## The passion machine

France play their rugby with great passion, what the Welsh call *hwyl*. Never was this quality more in evidence than during the 1999 World Cup semi-final against New Zealand, one of the greatest matches of all time, when they tailed 24–10 in the second half only to win 43–31 before a bedazzled Twickenham audience. When the charismatic French captain Raphael Ibanez was asked how on earth such a mesmeric turnaround had been possible, he replied with a typical Gallic shrug and said, 'Ehhh, we are French.'

Sometimes the French combine this passion with great aggression. One year they came to play their biannual fixture against Wales so intent on thumping everyone in a red jersey that a bodyguard was ordered for the Bishop of Cardiff up in the main stand.

## Chinese whispers

The great Welsh out-half Jonathan Davies once played in the Hong Kong Sevens. He decided he would go out for a real Chinese meal with Willie Anderson. After they had finished, Jonathan said he was going to do a runner. Willie told him not to be crazy, there were six guys at the door with machetes precisely to discourage people from leaving without paying their bill. Jonathan could do the 100 metres in about 10.5. Willie could do it in 16.5, so sprinting off was not a realistic option for him. When Jonathan ran out, Willie carefully considered his options. Eventually he took the decision and paid for both of them. When he went out, he found Jonathan hiding behind a dustbin!

One of the stories told about Jonathan's eye for a commercial opportunity goes back to when he was a child.

'Dad,' said Jonathan, 'when I grow up I want to be an Arctic explorer.'

'Fine, son,' replied his father.

'But I want to begin my training now.'

'But you're far too young, how can you do that?'

'Well, I want you to give me 20p a day for ice cream . . . so I can get used to the cold.'

## Soup-er star

Rob Howley tells the story of one of his international colleagues, hereafter called 'Player X' (the name has been changed to protect the guilty). He was selected in the squad for the Wales A v. England A game at Wrexham. Due to the long journey, the squad took a pit-stop in Welshpool for lunch and many ordered the soup of the day, including Player X. As the waitress was serving the soup to the squad, Player X decided to reach over and grab the condiments to shake onto his soup. The waitress, seeing him, kindly remarked, 'I would taste it first, love, if I was you.'

Player X shook the pepper onto his wrist and took a lick!

## Great Scott

When Scott Quinnell was 18, he was desperate to play his first match for Llanelli. He was on the bench and keen to get a run during a club match. He had dreamed about charging onto the field and playing for the club. There was an injury and Quinnell got the call to go on. His dream was about to be realised. He unzipped his tracksuit and stepped out, all ready to charge into battle. He knew instinctively something was wrong. He looked down and saw his socks and boots, but he was missing his shorts. He had dreamed of giving an eye-catching performance. He certainly succeeded.

## Like father, unlike son

Scott's father, Derek, was one of the stars of the great Welsh team of the 1970s. In the mid-'90s, when Scott had firmly established his reputation as a top player, both with Llanelli and in his incarnation as a rugby league player, Derek checked into a hotel. He was pleasantly surprised by the reaction of the hotel receptionist; when he signed the register, she said, 'Not *the* Mr Quinnell?'

'I'm Derek Quinnell who used to play for Wales.'

The receptionist did not attempt to hide her disappointment: 'Ah, I thought you might be Scott's father.'

## No, Prime Minister

The former Wales and Lions flanker John Taylor found a new career as ITV's chief rugby commentator. He was commentating on one of the worst international games of all time – the third-place play-off between England and France at the 1995 World Cup. Suddenly he got a message on his headphones about a major political story, which he was instructed to pass on to the nation. In an effort to face down his critics, John Major had sensationally announced he was going to stand down as leader of the Conservative Party and face any leadership challenge that might result. Taylor was told to say that ITV would continue with the game but as soon as it finished ITN's John Suchet would present a special bulletin. Hearing this news, Taylor's co-commentator said, 'Well, I know it's bad, John, but surely there's no need for the Prime Minister to resign over a game of rugby.'

## Choose wife

Llanelli and Wales legend Ieuan Evans was very dedicated to the game. Even after his retirement, his love for the game remains undiminished. To stress the point, the story is told of a conversation he had with his long-suffering wife: 'No, my dear – you must decide. After all, it's your birthday, not mine. Shall we go and see the England–Wales international, or the Llanelli–Cardiff game?'

## What happened next?

During the 1999–2000 season, Cardiff were playing arch rivals Newport at Cardiff Arms Park when Cardiff's Paul Burke faced a crucial conversion from the line in the dying moments. His team had just scored a try in the corner and they needed a conversion for victory. He placed the ball onto the carefully constructed pile of sand, walked back, looked at the post and steadied himself, deep in concentration, totally focused on the task at hand. Then a drunken supporter leapt over the advertising boards, sprinted over to the sideline and kicked the ball high into the stands to huge cheers. Stewards, policemen and the referee struggled to catch him. The biggest cheer of the night came when a policeman rugby-tackled him onto the muddy pitch. After all the disruption, Burke had to concentrate hard again to take the difficult kick. He did so successfully. After the match, a journalist asked him for his reaction to the incident. Ever the diplomat, Burke did not want to say anything to annoy the Newport fans so he replied, 'I don't comment whenever there's controversy. I've always believed that it's better to keep your mouth shut and appear stupid than to open it and remove all doubt.'

The kicking supporter had been wearing a sweatshirt with 'Carlsberg' on it. His fellow Newport fans were less reticent than Burke and said, 'He's probably the greatest rugby player in the world!'

Newport and Cardiff fans enjoy a keen rivalry and swap jokes at each other's expense. After Cardiff sustained a bad loss in the Heineken Cup, a Newport fan said, 'The only way Cardiff can get up again is with Viagra.'

In retaliation, Cardiff fans came up with a new joke of their own:

Q: What do you say to a Newport person on Cup final day?
A: Two bars of chocolate, please.

## The fast Lane

Rugby players like to employ mind games to try and outpsyche their opponents. Sometimes their plans backfire. Stuart Lane prided himself on the fact that the tougher it got, the better he liked it. During internationals, he was well able to verbally intimidate opponents. The best example of this was when Ireland played Wales in 1980. Where in Ireland's Colin Patterson's anatomy Lane was going to stuff the ball cannot be repeated in polite society. Patterson eventually turned around and said to him, 'Stuart, you don't mean that.' Stuart burst into laughter and said, 'You're a cheeky wee bollocks.'

# Welsh Wit

## Not over the Cliff

Bill Shankly's famous saying that football is not a matter of life or death but more important applies to rugby in Wales. Rugby is to the Welsh what films are to Hollywood: a universal obsession that sets a pecking order, discussed endlessly and by everyone, complete with its own arcane laws and rituals. Pubs are the churches of this strange sporting religion and its gurus are anyone who can hold an audience. This art's greatest prince is Cliff Morgan.

One of his favourite stories is about the two Welsh fans sitting at the bar, reliving the latest game they had seen. After a brief lull in the conversation, one said to the other, 'I wonder if there's rugby in heaven?' His friend said that nobody knew for sure, but suggested that they should make a pact there and then that whichever of them died first would come back and tell the other. They both agreed and the pact was soon sealed with another round of drinks. In due course, one of the men died and the day after being buried he turned up at the foot of his friend's bed as arranged. The man in the bed almost died himself with fright but soon remembered the purpose of the visit. He sat up immediately, eager to hear the news. 'Tell me quick,' he said. 'Is there rugby in heaven?'

The dead man replied, 'Well, I have good news and I have bad news. The good news is that, yes, there's rugby in heaven all right. But the bad news is that there's a game next Saturday and you're playing scrum-half.'

Cliff has a way with words. Asked to describe a prop forward, he said he 'looked very strong'. That meant that he was about 18 stone!

Even Cliff, though, had his off-days in the commentary box: 'Sadly, the immortal Jackie Milburn died recently.'

The one mystery about rugby that Cliff could never figure out was the selection policies pursued by Welsh universities, the classic example being the case of a player who was picked once for a Welsh university that will remain nameless, scored three tries and was dropped for the next match. The next year he was selected again, scored four tries and was dropped again.

Morgan was not the only Welsh legend called Cliff. On the Lions tour of 1950, the great character was Cliff Davies, a Welsh coalminer. Cliff was a larger-than-life figure. He was greeted by the New Zealand Prime Minister, S.G. Holland, who said: 'Glad to meet you, Cliff.'

Cliff retorted, 'Glad to meet you, Sid.'

Cliff was once asked his opinion of a young minister ordained in his local village on a Thursday night. He played second-row forward for the local team on the Saturday and everyone went to hear him preach his first sermon on the following Sunday morning. As he left the church, Cliff was asked what he thought of the new pastor. Cliff replied, 'Powerful in prayer but hopeless in the lineout.'

## The man in the middle

There have been few more famous referees in the history of rugby than Neath's Clive Norling. Norling's favourite story is about a headstone in a cemetery in Swansea. It stands over the grave of Thomas William Griffiths James. The inscription reads: 'Here lies an honest man and a referee.'

Clive's punchline is: 'So that proves that we can bury two in the same grave in Wales.'

Clive was refereeing a game and called over a prop forward who was gouging in a ruck. Clive was about to admonish him sternly but began by simply asking him his name. The prop replied, 'Rachid Hazerbichaek.'

Clive gulped and simply said, 'Well, don't do that again.'

## Rest in peace

When a former Welsh player dies, there is invariably a massive attendance by sports personalities at the funeral. These occasions are generally a celebration of a life lived. Stories are swapped about great games, players and characters, and great compliments and insults are lovingly traded about players living and dead. A good example would be Frank Keating's view that 'John Bevan [the winger who starred on the great Welsh team of the '70s] could jink like a crazed pinball and hare like a barmy rabbit.' This would be immediately countered by Arthur Clues' observation on Bevan: 'As bald as a coot. Not a tooth in his head. A skeleton in braces.'

Funerals for other sports stars are more fraught, notably the funeral of the Welsh boxer, Tommy Farr. Tommy had fought Joe Louis for the world title in 1937 and had been destroyed, but he was such a hero in Wales that the Welsh all claimed he was robbed. When he died, his funeral service was attended almost exclusively by ex-boxers with severely disfigured noses and cauliflower ears, and a lot of them were in a pretty bad mental state, sparring with themselves. The minister was afraid of a riot and before the service started he called over the altar boy and said, 'Brown, whatever I say and whatever I do, don't ring that bell or they'll start the mother of all fights.'

## Foreplay

At a dull party a middle-aged man approached a very attractive young woman with an unusual proposition. 'Would you chat to me for a minute or two? Cardiff are playing on television tonight and if my wife sees me talking to you she'll decide that it's time to go home.'

## Cold comfort

A winger was playing in a charity match in Newport. It was a bitterly cold day. By the time the game was over his wife, watching in the stands, was absolutely frozen. As she reached for her thermos and unscrewed the lid, she told her friend: 'There's only one thing to warm you up on a day like today.' Then she took out a pair of clean socks – still warm from the tumble-drier.

# Odd-Shaped Balls

## Them and us

In rugby, the enemy is generally England, as Max Boyce demonstrated in this unique vision of the Last Judgement.

> When it comes to the one great scorer
> To mark against your name,
> He'll not ask you how you played the game,
> But whether you beat England!

On one famous occasion, the crowds had been gathering since lunch-time in Cardiff Arms Park for the game with England. One of the first into the stand was a man who had presented two tickets on arrival. With only five minutes to go before the match, the seat beside him remained unoccupied. This aroused the curiosity of the person on his other side. 'Are you waiting on someone?' he enquired.

'Ah, no,' replied the fan. 'We've had a death in the family since I bought the tickets. In fact, to tell you the truth, it was my wife that died.'

'I'm very sorry for your trouble,' said the other, 'but couldn't you get someone else from the family to come along with you?'

'No, they all wanted to go to her funeral!'

There is a famous story about a Welsh rugby team at Cardiff Arms Park. For 20 minutes, ankle-deep in mud, the forwards hardly released the ball from the scrum for a moment. At last it emerged to the scrum-half, who passed to the fly-half, who then kicked it high over the grandstand. A search party set off to look for it and after ten minutes had not returned. One of the Welsh pack – or it might have been the English – was heard to say, 'Never mind the ruddy ball, let's get on with the ruddy game.'

Some pleasures, like marrying a woman for love and later discovering that she has lots of money, creep up as surprises. Others are much more predictable. A recurring theme in most chapters in this book is the way the various countries react to beating England. The attitude was perhaps best summed up by French international Imanol Harinordoquy before France played England in the Six Nations in 2003: 'I despise them as much as they despise everybody else. And as long as we beat England I wouldn't mind if we lost every other game in the Six Nations.' France lost and England went on to win the Grand Slam.

In Wales, beating England is the ultimate in rugby terms. A man approached the pearly gates and was asked by St Peter whether he had ever done anything wrong. 'I was a rugby referee,' said the man, 'and when I was refereeing an international match between Wales and England at Cardiff Arms Park, I wrongly awarded a try to England when one of their players had committed an infringement.'

'That doesn't sound too bad,' said St Peter, 'if that is all you have done. How long ago did this happen?'

'About 30 seconds ago,' said the man.

English fans get their revenge with a story emphasising the decline in Welsh rugby fortunes since the glory days of the 1970s. A naval boiler-stoker and fanatical Wales fan goes to Hell. The Devil comes up to him on the first day and sees him smiling. 'What are you so happy about?' asks the Devil.

'I just love it here. It's like a spring day in the boiler room.'

Lucifer is furious and thinks to himself that he's going to make him suffer. He says to himself, 'I'm going to turn the heat all the way up. That'll show him.'

The following day, the Devil checks back with the Welsh fan only to find him still beaming.

Again the prince of darkness asks why the fan is so happy. 'This heat is great! Reminds me of a summer day in the boiler room.'

The Devil realises that he has been going about it all wrong. 'Tomorrow I'm going to make it colder than a Siberian winter.'

He turns up the next day to find the stoker shivering and blue, but grinning from ear to ear.

'What could you possibly have to be happy about?'

'It's pretty obvious, isn't it?' answered the stoker. 'Wales must have won the Grand Slam!'

## Back to basics

A Welsh junior club side went on a tour of the Scottish Highlands. They were booked in to a small hotel. The players knew what was in store for them as soon as they walked in the front door and read a notice: 'To call room service – open the door and call room service.'

## Uncertainty

A Welsh club team were on a tour of Ireland. They were being driven down from Dublin to Cork. On the way, they came to a level-crossing at a railway station whose gate was halfway across the road. The team waited patiently for ten minutes and then the bus driver got out and found the stationmaster and asked, 'Do you know the gate is halfway across the road?'

'I do,' replied the stationmaster. 'We're half expecting the train from Cork.'

## Practice makes perfect

A Welsh club team was on tour in France. One of their second-rows was big but not too bright, and the team was always ribbing him about his sex life. 'Is it true, Jones,' he was asked in the changing-room one day, 'that you've been trying out lots of new sexual positions?'

'I certainly have,' said Jones enthusiastically. 'I'm getting good, too! The next thing is to try them out with girls!'

# FOUR

# When Irish Eyes Are Smiling

### The Life of Brian

The star of the Irish team is Brian O'Driscoll, whose stature in the game was confirmed when Sir Clive Woodward appointed him captain of the Lions touring party in 2005. Brian has been in thrall to the game of rugby for as long as he can remember. It helps that his father Frank played for Ireland and that his cousins Barry and John also played for their country. Ours is an age wedded to an almost mystical concept of celebrity. Brian's mother Geraldine is all too aware of this. The France game in 2000, when he scored the three tries, changed everything for Brian and indeed for his family. Geraldine first realised this when she was introduced to someone after the match with the words, 'This is Geraldine O'Driscoll. She used to be Frank O'Driscoll's wife. Now she's Brian O'Driscoll's mother.'

The game was on a Sunday, and shortly after the match Frank and Geraldine had to rush for the train to be home for work the next day. One of their daughters was in Australia at the time and she rang them on the mobile. She said, 'Mum, after Brian's three tries I'm now a minor celebrity here!'

Geraldine really noticed just how famous Brian had become the following Halloween. She knew there would be lots of kids calling to the house trick or treating. She put piles of sweets on the table and left Brian in charge of them. When she came back, she was shocked to find all the sweets still there and to see a bundle of pieces of paper lying beside the sweets. She asked Brian what had happened and he replied, 'The doorbell hasn't stopped ringing all evening but none of the kids want the sweets. They just want my autograph.'

After his hat-trick of tries for Ireland against France, O'Driscoll's nickname became 'God'. When Brian scored his sensational try for the Lions against Australia in the First Test in 2001, Stuart Barnes observed, 'They call him God. Well, I reckon he's a better player than that.'

Everybody loves a winner. In 2001, the Irish rugby team got an audience with the Pope when they travelled to Rome to play Italy. Injury forced O'Driscoll to miss the trip. The late Pope John Paul II on his death bed was said to have only one regret – that he never got the chance to meet Brian O'Driscoll!

## Denis the Menace
O'Driscoll captained Ireland to only her seventh Triple Crown in March 2004. In recent years, Drico has enjoyed a good-natured rivalry with Ireland's flying winger Denis Hickie as they yo-yoed in the race to be Ireland's record-breaking try-scorer. O'Driscoll grabbed the record off Hickie with his 24th try for Ireland, against Italy. After the match, Drico received a text message from Hickie: 'I suppose I should maybe, perhaps, congratulate you on your new record. Bollocks!'

## When Irish Eyes Are Smiling

### Fast Eddie

Part of rugby culture is that everyone has a nickname. Irish coach Eddie O'Sullivan, though, breaks the mould because he's got no less than three nicknames. After the controversial dismissal in 2002 of Warren Gatland as Ireland's rugby coach, Eddie succeeded him in one of the most high-pressure jobs in Irish sport. As a player, Eddie lined out on the wing with Garryowen and he was pretty quick, so Neil Francis in the *Sunday Tribune* calls him 'Fast Eddie'. Eddie trained as a PE teacher in Limerick and played a lot of indoor soccer there. As he was a very incisive player he got the nickname 'the Dagger'. Since his alleged role in the dismissal of Warren Gatland people have used that name against him in a different context! When he went to Garryowen, he did a lot of weight training, which was very unusual in the 1970s, though now it's par for the course in rugby. His teammates didn't think he was doing weights for rugby reasons, so they called him 'the Beach Boy'.

O'Sullivan may have been a little surprised when Keith Wood said after his retirement, 'I think I'll take a step away from the game for a while. I don't have the temperament to be a coach. I've known that for a while. Eddie may be a cranky man but he's not quite as cranky as I am.'

### Water, water everywhere

The Irish swimming fraternity has long been waiting for an Olympic-size pool. In 2002, the IRFU began the first phase of construction of its new pitch at Lansdowne Road. Ireland played autumn internationals against both Australia and Argentina during downpours. The pitch was covered in water in many places and barely playable. One swimming fan watching the Argentina match from the stands remarked, 'Congratulations to the IRFU in giving us our first-ever 100-metre swimming-pool.'

## Odd-Shaped Balls

### Ulster says yes

In 1999, Ulster won the European Cup final at Lansdowne Road. All of Ireland got behind Ulster, who were bidding to become the first Irish side to win the competition. A number of prominent Ulster Unionist politicians were at Lansdowne Road for the occasion. One found himself in the proximity of a staunch republican who was very much on the opposite end of the spectrum in terms of attitude to Northern Ireland. The unionist turned to this fervent nationalist and said, 'How does it feel to belong to a 32-County Ulster?'

### Winging it

The late Mick Doyle was not a man to lavish praise on the Irish team with wanton abandon, so when he described an Irish victory as an '80-minute orgasm', one had to sit up and take notice. The performance which prompted this vintage 'Doylerism' was Ireland's 17–3 victory over England in 1993.

Still basking in the glory of their win over the All Blacks, the English expected to extract retribution at Twickenham in 1994, but a splendid try from Simon Geoghegan helped Ireland to secure another shock win – this time on a score of 13–12. During these years, the Underwood brothers played on the wings for England. Whenever either scored a try, the director of the BBC coverage of the game always cut to the stands, where invariably their mother was dancing a jig with elation. After scything past Tony Underwood to score that try, Simon is said to have turned to Underwood and remarked, 'I hope your mother saw that!'

Another famous quip is former Irish international Trevor Brennan's remark to referee Alan Lewis: 'It's not a sin bin you need, it's a skip.'

### A ripe, old age

In 1985, after Ireland famously beat England to win the Triple Crown, Willie Anderson's wife Heather met the wife of the Nobel Prize-winning poet Seamus Heaney, which was a big thrill for her as she is an English teacher. A few weeks afterwards they were at the dinner to mark the Triple Crown victory. It was the night of one of Barry McGuigan's big fights and Willie went upstairs to see the contest on the television. Heather was left on her own and was trying to make polite conversation. She was chatting to Ciaran Fitzgerald and made a bit of a faux pas by telling him that she had met James Joyce's wife after the England match. Fitzie turned around and asked Hugo MacNeill what age Mrs Joyce would be. Hugo answered, 'About 150!'

## The French connection

After Ireland won the Triple Crown in 1982, Ireland travelled to France hoping to win the Grand Slam. The Irish team bus entered the stadium and was surrounded by French supporters who were going crazy, thumping the side of the bus and shouting abuse at the team. The Irish team was very tense and everyone was silent. Donal Lenihan was sitting beside Moss Finn. The French fans were screaming: *'L'Irlande est fini. L'Irlande est fini.'*

Moss stood up and said, 'Christ, lads. Isn't it great to be recognised?'

In his early days with Ireland, Donal usually roomed with Moss Keane. Moss was coming to the end of his career at that stage; their room was like an alternative medical centre with pollen, garlic tablets and half a dozen eggs. The mornings of internationals, Donal always awoke to see Moss eating three raw eggs. It's not the sort of sight that you want to wake up to.

## Better bad days

In 1981, Ireland lost all four matches in the Five Nations, each time by a single score, after leading in each match at half-time. It was Ireland's best-ever whitewash.

## Doyler

Mick Doyle famously coached Ireland to the Triple Crown in 1985. Although he played on his 'give-it-a-lash' image, he was a very shrewd coach. Before getting the Ireland job, he was coach of Leinster. The province played Romania when they toured Ireland in 1980. The home side arrived at the ground well over an hour before the game; the players thought they had mistimed the arrival. However, the previous week Romania had hammered Munster, and Doyler had noticed that in the lead-up to the match the Romanian players were constantly in and out of the toilet. Being the cute Kerry man that he was, Doyler gave a newspaper and a match programme to each of the Leinster substitutes and told them to lock themselves in the toilets until the game began. Leinster demolished the Romanians in the match. The next day the phrase that was used in the newspapers was 'The Romanians were strangely heavy and leaden-footed.' Was it any surprise?

After his career as Irish coach ended, Mick Doyle wrote his autobiography, which was described by one observer as a 'good love guide'. He rang up the Irish Prime Minister Charlie Haughey to see if he would be willing to help launch the book. Haughey asked him what it was about. Doyle said, '20 per cent is about rugby and 80 per cent is pornography.' The then Prime Minister said, 'You got the balance just right!' Charlie opened his speech on the night by saying, 'I always like people who expose themselves in public.'

At one of Mick's book signings, a few men arrived dressed up as nuns. One of the scenes in the book relates how Doyler was caught in a state of undress by a nun after performing the 'marital act'.

Some time later he was doing a book signing in O'Mahony's Bookshop in Limerick. Former Irish Prime Minister Garrett FitzGerald had been there the night before promoting his autobiography. In the front window they had photographs of both Doyle and FitzGerald. As he prepared for his signing, Doyler noticed a religious brother in his white collar walking up and down past the shop shouting, 'Get that b*****d out the window.' One of the shop assistants went out and asked him, 'What's wrong with Mick Doyle?'

'Nothing. He's a grand fella. It's that other so-and-so that I can't stand!'

There was some very hostile reaction to Mick's book, as it recounted in vivid detail some of his sexual conquests. Doyle claimed that the best story he heard about it was about two women in a taxi who were discussing it. One said, 'I can't understand how anybody could write a book like that while they were still alive.'

There was some suggestion that Doyler must have added to some of the stories about his off-the-field activities in his autobiography. One of the players who knew him best, Jim Glennon, disagreed. His feeling would be that, if anything, they were probably slightly understated!

## The good, the glad and Ollie

No Irish sports star apart from George Best has filled more newspaper columns than Tony Ward. Ward exploded onto the sporting scene in 1978 when he first played for Ireland. He was already a local hero in Limerick, where he was training to be a PE teacher in Thomond College, because of his displays for one of the city's top teams, Garryowen.

Ward was the unnamed culprit in a story that did the rounds just as he broke into the Irish team. The story involved two conversations between a Young Munster (Garryowen's great rivals) supporter and his parish priest.

Priest: 'Tis a long time since your face has been seen in this sacred house, my son. Anyway we cater for all types here. Can I be of any assistance to you at all?

Fan: I don't know if you can, Father. You see this could be a job for the bishop. I'm in an awful way. My state of mind is such that all communications with the wife, both verbal and otherwise, have temporarily ceased.

Priest: My son, confession is good for the soul. What is the terrible secret that you bear?

Fan: Father, the truth is . . . I . . . I . . . am in danger of becoming a supporter of the Garryowen team.

Priest: I see. That's bad. In fact, it's very bad.

Fan: I knew you would understand, Father. All my life I thought that rugby consisted of rucks, scrums and lineouts with a few fights thrown in for good measure. Where I come from, shouts of 'ahead, ahead' have a different meaning from that understood elsewhere. To be candid, Father, I was happy in my ignorance, but now 'tis all jinking and running, reverse-passing and blind-side moves. And to make matters worse, Father, I am being entertained by it all. Tell me . . . Do you think I could be losing the faith?

Priest: My son, the ordinary, everyday problems of life – wife-swapping, divorce, drinking – are but minor problems compared to your dilemma. Come back to me tomorrow, I shall have spoken with a higher authority by then.

The next day . . .

Priest: My son, you can put your mind to rest. A solution to your problem exists and where else was it to be found but in . . . religion. Within a year or two, the blackguard most responsible for Garryowen's madness and for your unhappy state of mind will be plucked from our midst and transported away. Normality will return.

Fan: But how can I be sure of this?

Priest: My son, the bells of St Mary's will ring out for him . . . and he will answer their call.

Shortly afterwards Ward transferred to St Mary's club in Dublin.

Playing for Ireland, Ward struck up an instant rapport with his half-back partner Colin Patterson, on and off the field. 'Patty' went on Ireland's leading television programme *The*

*Late, Late Show* with Tony when Ward was the golden boy of Irish rugby, and landed him in big trouble. Wardie was involved in a serious relationship at the time and the presenter Gay Byrne asked him if he had a girlfriend. Patty immediately quipped, 'One in every town.' Tony had a lot of explaining to do to his young lady after that!

## Campbell's kingdom

After he was sensationally dropped by the Irish rugby selectors on the tour to Australia in 1979, Tony Ward became embroiled in one of the most keenly argued controversies in the history of Irish sport. For three years a fierce debate raged: who should wear Ireland's number 10 jersey – Ward or Ollie Campbell?

Ollie Campbell thought he had finally resolved the Tony Ward issue with a series of stunning performances that ensured Ireland broke a 33-year famine and won the Triple Crown in 1982. A few weeks later, Ollie was leaving Westport one morning when he picked up an oldish lady who was thumbing a lift to visit a friend in Castlebar Hospital. After an initial flurry of small talk the conversation unfolded as follows:

Her: And what sports do you play? Do you play Gaelic?

Ollie (as modestly as possible): No, I play rugby.

Long silence.

Her: Do you know, there's one thing I'll never understand about rugby.

Ollie (with all due modesty): What? I might be able to help.

Short silence.

Her: The only thing I don't understand about rugby is why Tony Ward isn't on the Irish team.

In 1984, Ollie found himself the main topic of conversation among the chattering classes. When he pulled out of the England game in 1984, it was suggested by some that he was giving up rugby and joining the priesthood! He has absolutely no idea where this particular rumour emanated from. To this day, though, former Irish scrum-half John Robbie still calls him Father Campbell. Two weeks later, after Ireland played Scotland, in order to highlight just how absurd that fabricated story was, Ollie turned up dressed as a priest at the post-match dinner. Not only that, he persuaded a female friend of his to accompany him dressed up as a nun. He went around all night with a fag in one hand (he has never smoked) and a pint in the other (and at the time he didn't drink) and danced away with this 'nun', although he has never been much of a dancer. All of this was so out of character for him that he assumed that people would immediately see that the priesthood story was entire nonsense. What staggered him was the amount of people who came up to him and, apologising to 'sister' for interrupting, sincerely congratulated him on his big decision! Instead of putting this little fire out, all he succeeded in doing was to pour fuel on it.

Even after his retirement from rugby Campbell still found his name linked with Tony Ward's. He was invited to appear on Mike Murphy's radio show at one stage. Before the broadcast, he was asked if there were any subjects he did not wish to discuss. He said, 'Tony Ward and South Africa' because he thought they had been flogged to death. The first question Mike asked him was: 'I see here, Ollie, that the two areas that you've said you do not want to be questioned about are South Africa and Tony Ward. Why is that?'

Ollie was at a meal in the Oyster Tavern in Cork after Munster played the All Blacks in 1989 and he sat down beside a great stalwart of the Greystones club, Eric Cole. He was aware that when he did so some people started whispering and nudging each other. He continued talking away to Eric and they had a great chat but there were a lot of comments being made which were going straight over his head, like 'Ollie, give Wardie a break.' It was only afterwards he discovered that Tony had being going out with Eric's daughter Louise for months, and they got engaged shortly after that. Afterwards some typical Greystones mischief-makers put out the story that, not being content to 'steal' Wardie's place on the Irish team, Ollie was now also trying to steal his girlfriend!

## Patty

Lions scrum-half Colin Patterson made his international debut against the All Blacks in 1978. Patterson was a rugby ecumenicist, singing the national anthem with gusto before matches even though he was not from nationalist stock. Tony Ward taught him the first six or seven lines of the anthem and then he discovered that he could sing it to the tune of the unionist anthem 'The Sash'. He sang the first half of 'The Soldier's Song' and the second half of 'The Sash' just to give it political balance!

Patty was a big admirer of Ollie Campbell's dedication. When Ollie Campbell came into the Irish squad, he and Mike Gibson would stay on the pitch on their own for extra training. Patty claims that since they didn't drink they had nothing else to do.

## Supermac

One of Campbell's closest friends on the Irish team was Hugo MacNeill. Capped 37 times for Ireland, Hugo scored eight international tries, a record for a full-back, making him perhaps Ireland's greatest attacking full-back of all time. When he burst onto the Irish team, he was in awe of Willie Duggan. In 1985, following Duggan's retirement, their relationship was more like that between equals. Hugo promised to get Willie tickets for the Scotland match. He was sharing a room with Brian Spillane and the phone rang the night before the match. Hugo answered with the words 'The Spillane–MacNeill suite'.

Immediately, he heard Willie respond, 'You might as well be sleeping together, you spend so much time together on the pitch!'

Ireland's form in the post-Mick Doyle era slumped dramatically, culminating in a humiliating 35–3 defeat at

Twickenham in 1988. At least the match generated one of the most celebrated stories in recent Irish rugby folklore. MacNeill went AWOL during the game. Although Ireland went in with a 3–0 lead at half-time, they were slaughtered in the second half. When the second half started, Hugo was not there and nobody knew where he was. Ollie Campbell's joke after the game was that MacNeill went in to make a phone call. By the time he came back onto the pitch they had run in for two tries.

Hugo did get his own back on Campbell, though. Ollie's biggest problem is that he can't say no when people ask him to do them a favour. Hugo rang him up one night, put on an accent and told him he was Mick Fitzgerald from Irish Marketing Ltd and was organising a beauty competition for nurses, and that he wanted him to be one of the judges, knowing full well that Ollie would hate that kind of thing. He sighed and sighed, struggling to come up with a plausible excuse. Eventually Ollie asked what date the contest was. When Hugo gave him the date, Ollie said, 'Oh, that's an awful shame. I'm really sorry but I have another function on that night. It's such a pity because I always wanted to judge a beauty contest.'

'That's no problem, Ollie. You see, one of the prizes we're going to offer is a night out with Ollie Campbell. We'll pay for everything and it'll be first class all the way.'

'Gosh, I'm afraid I'm going to have a lot of commitments around that time. I won't have many nights free.'

'But that's the beauty of this, Ollie, we'll arrange it for any night that suits you.'

The panic was getting ever more noticeable in Ollie's voice and Hugo could visualise him writhing in his chair as he tried to find a way to back out of it. Eventually, Ollie said he was backing away from that type of thing. Then Hugo asked him if there were any of his colleagues who would be willing to do that kind of thing. Ollie blurted out Hugo's name immediately and provided his phone number faster than you could say Tony Ward!

## A rolling stone gathers no . . .

Stories about Moss Keane are more common than showers in April – though few are printable in our politically correct times. Some are even true. Moss has a nice line in self-deprecating humour: 'After I left university, I found I had no talent for anything so I joined the civil service'; 'I won 52 caps – a lot of them just because they couldn't find anybody else.'

Tony Ward and Mick Quinn once both got 18 points in a final trial for Ireland, but Quinn felt he had outplayed Ward on the day and was feeling pretty good. Moss Keane came up to Quinn at the reception that night and told him that he was the best out-half he had ever played with. He was pretty chuffed with the compliment and told him so. Shortly after, he was on his way to the toilet when he saw Mossie talking to somebody, but he couldn't make out who it was at first. As he passed them, he realised it was Wardie and he heard Mossie tell him he was without doubt the finest out-half ever to play for Ireland. Quinn gave him a kick in the backside for his dishonesty. Mossie followed him into the toilet, put his arm around him and said, 'Don't worry, Scout. I was only being diplomatic.'

When the troubles in the North were at their height, Lansdowne played a match in Belfast. After the match, the lads stopped for a case of beer in an off-licence because the drink was so much cheaper up there; this would set them up nicely for the train journey home. That evening, though, there was a bomb scare, which ruled out travelling by train, and after a long delay a bus arrived instead. The problem was that there was no room on the bus for Moss and some of the other players. Moss had already disposed of a couple of his beers and was not too happy with the prospect of having to wait even longer. He marched onto the bus and according to folklore said, 'Excuse me, this bus is going to crash.' At first nobody moved, but then a little old man got up and walked up timidly to the towering figure of Moss and said, 'Excuse me, sir, but where did you say this bus was going to?'

Moss was once asked to give an after-dinner speech at very short notice. He began by saying that he felt like a dog surrounded by four trees – he didn't have a leg to stand on.

## Labour of love

One of Keane's teammates for a period was Dick Spring, who for much of the 1980s and 1990s was Ireland's deputy Prime Minister. In 1979, Spring was capped three times for Ireland at rugby.

He is probably best remembered, though unfairly, as he was a much better player than he was given credit for, for an incident in a Wales match when Ireland gifted the home side 15 points, to lose on a scoreline of 24–21. After 22 minutes, Ireland led 6–0, courtesy of two lengthy penalties from Tony Ward. In the 25th minute, the picture changed dramatically. The Welsh fly-half lofted the kick towards the Irish posts but Spring was under it and there seemed to be no danger. Somehow the ball slipped through his hands and bounced over the Irish line for Allan Martin to rush on and score a try which Steve Fenwick converted. While his political career flourished in the 1980s and 1990s, he has never been allowed to forget that incident and has been the butt of jokes about 'a safe pair of hands' ever since. Throughout the enormously popular series on RTE, *Radio One Scrap Saturday*, Spring was consistently referred to by Dermot Morgan, who went on to find fame as Father Ted, as 'Butterfingers'. As a result, Spring always claims that the highlight of his career was his first cap against France. That's the game he shows to his kids. He claims he can't remember what happened in the Wales game!

John Major was quite impressed when he heard Spring had played for Ireland. Major played rugby himself when he was very young but didn't prosper at the game because at that time he was too small, even though he's a tall man now. Major's great passion is cricket and his moods fluctuated a lot depending on the fate of the English team. Spring was always wary about entering into sensitive negotiations with Major about the peace process in Northern Ireland when England were playing. He found the best time to negotiate with Major was when England were doing very well at cricket. The only problem was that that didn't happen very often.

One trick Spring used to get the attention of a rugby audience in Wales was to give the first three minutes of his speech in Irish. By the time he started speaking in English, they were ready to hang on his every word!

## Captain Marvel

Stories about Willie Duggan abound. Like Moss Keane, he was an Irish national institution. A man with little enthusiasm for training, his most celebrated comment was, 'Training takes the edge off my game.' Duggan was one of a rare group of players who always made a point of bringing a pack of cigarettes with him onto the training field. Asked once in a radio interview if this was a major problem for him fitness-wise, he took the broadcaster by surprise by saying that it was a positive advantage: 'Sure, if it wasn't for the fags I would be offside all day long.'

There was an inherent contradiction in Duggan's preparation for matches. He always had a cigarette five minutes before going out on the pitch, then he took out a jar of Vicks and rubbed it on his chest. To put it at its kindest, he had an unconventional approach!

Willie was finding it difficult to make it to training with his club team, Blackrock, in Dublin. It was agreed, at Irish hooker John Cantrell's suggestion, that one Sunday the entire squad would go down to Kilkenny Rugby Club to make life easier for Willie, because he lived there. That morning they were all there apart from guess who? Willie! Somebody had to go and wake him because he had slept in.

Donal Lenihan tells another story about Willie Duggan.

Donal considers Willie the Scarlet Pimpernel of Irish rugby because he was so hard to find for training. During his reign as Irish captain Willie was not known for his gentle words of encouragement to his players. One of Donal's clearest memories of Willie's captaincy is of the morning after the Scotland game in 1984 when all the papers had a picture of Duggan with his arm around Tony Ward, speaking to him. It was just before Ward was taking a penalty. It looked like Willie was acting the real father-figure but, knowing him as Donal does, his guess is that Willie was saying, 'If you miss this penalty, I'll kick you all the way to Kilkenny.'

## Amazing Grace
Tom Grace had a very different approach to the Irish captaincy from Duggan.

When Grace played rugby, he had jet black hair and a Beatles haircut so it came as an enormous shock to him when his hair went grey. He was up in Donegal with his family before one of the international matches. RTE were showing some footage of tries from previous seasons. When they started to show a few of Grace's, his wife rushed out to call their son, Conor, who was six at the time, to see his dad in his prime. When Conor came in, she pointed to the television excitedly and showed Grace in full flight. Conor just shook his head and said, 'No, it's not him. My dad has grey hair.' Then he just turned on his heels and ran out to play soccer.

One of the captains of the Univesity College Dublin side Grace played on was Peter Sutherland, who became a giant in the business and economic world after he was made European Commissioner in the 1980s. 'Suds' put his own stamp on the captaincy. The nights before the Cup matches the UCD players met at his house in Monkstown. A walk on Dun Laoghaire pier became part of the ritual. For the first match they had sandwiches, tea, coffee and soft drinks. As their Cup run progressed, the refreshments became ever more lavish.

# When Irish Eyes Are Smiling

The night before the semi-final, they had a totally fabulous dinner with all kinds of delicacies. Then Suds gave his speech. The food was incredibly memorable. The speech wasn't. The next day UCD lost narrowly . . . 28–3!

## Moloney's memories

Tom Grace was succeeded as Irish captain by his clubmate Johnny Moloney. Johnny was a very single-minded player. In a schoolboy match, he was charging through for a try when a despairing dive by his marker robbed him of his shorts. True to form, he raced through for the try in his underpants before worrying about getting new togs.

## The Mighty Quinn

Mick Quinn enjoyed his rivalry with Ollie Campbell and Tony Ward for the Irish number 10 jersey. In his autobiography, *The Good, The Bad and the Rugby*, Ward jokes that if it wasn't for Ollie Campbell he would have got 40 caps. When Quinn read that, he rang Tony and said if it wasn't for Ward, Mike Gibson, Barry McGann, Ollie and Paul Dean he would have won 80 caps.

One of the highlights of Quinn's career was winning the three-in-a-row of Leinster Cups in 1981 with Lansdowne. They beat Old Belvedere in the final and it was nice to put one over on Ollie Campbell on the pitch. After the match, the team bus was bringing the Lansdowne team on to the victory celebrations. Quinn suggested to his colleagues they should 'lob a moon', or display their bums out the window, to the people of Dublin. This proposal was enthusiastically agreed to. When they were on display, Quinn turned around and saw there was a car travelling alongside the bus. To his horror, the occupants were his father, mother and sister. His mother told him afterwards that she had recognised his bum because it hadn't changed since the time she used to change his nappies! Quinn told her he found that hard to believe.

Perhaps Quinn's most enduring legacy to the rugby landscape is the number of players he has given nicknames to.

He called former international scrum-half Tony Doyle 'Gandhi' because there was more meat in a cheese sandwich. He called the Wesley player Dave Priestman 'Vicarman' because, he told him, it was ridiculous for a Protestant to be called priest. He called Brendan Mullin 'Bugs Bunny' because of his smile. He also christened Harry Steele 'Stainless' for obvious reasons; Rory Underwood 'the Chinese Takeaway' and Jean-Pierre Rives, now a noted sculptor, and the living proof that you don't have to be big to be a world-class forward, 'Je t'aime' because he had such charm with women.

Quinn claims the credit for Mike Gibson's great displays for Ireland. Mick always blessed himself with Lourdes water before matches; he always splashed some on Gibson's legs when he wasn't looking and Gibbo went out and played like a genius.

Quinn was such a prankster that any time he passed on a message, people got suspicious. At one stage he came into the dressing-room before a match against Wales and said to Tony Ward, 'There's a strange-looking auld fella out there who wants a word with you.' Knowing Quinn's reputation, Ward was very apprehensive and also wanted to prepare for the match. He told Quinn not to be annoying him or a more colourful variation of it. Eventually he agreed to go out, but with some trepidation. Who was there simply just to shake his hand and say how much he admired him as a player? Neil Kinnock.

## Johnny come lately

Quinn has a particular affection for another former Irish international – as much for his off-the-field activities as for his playing career. Johnny Murphy was a great captain of Leinster. He has a bus and hearse business and turned up for training one night in his hearse with a coffin inside. Some of the Leinster players found it disconcerting to be doing their press-ups beside a coffin and grumbled to Johnny. He just said, 'She's not going anywhere and doesn't mind waiting.'

Johnny's speeches were memorable, not least because he was

great at taking off posh accents. His opening sentence after a Connacht match was, 'Mr President of Leinster, Mr President of Connacht, players and the rest of you hangers-on.'

The next week Leinster played Llanelli and beat the pants off them. Everyone was dying to know what Johnny would say. He began, 'Well, lads, I've got to be very careful what I say this week. It was a great honour for us to have the privilege of playing against such a famous side. My only regret is that BBC's *Rugby Special* wasn't here to see us beating the sh*te out of ye. I know people will say ye were missing some of yer star players but don't forget we were missing one of our greatest stars – Hugo MacNeill. He couldn't get his f**king place – I have it.' The whole place was in stitches and Ray Gravell in particular had to be picked off the floor, he was laughing so hard.

## Adventurous spirit
As Irish captain, Fergus Slattery had an unusual motivational style. Before Ireland played Wales at Cardiff Arms Park in 1979, Fergus brought the team to see *Adventures of a Window Cleaner* and *Adventures of a Taxi Driver*. Those films certainly took the players' minds off the game!

Fergus and his clubmate Willie Duggan played hard on and off the pitch. The difference was that whereas Fergus never seemed to show any ill-effects the next day, Willie did. It was an accepted fact that Willie came last at every exercise in training. Every player's recurring nightmare was that Duggan would beat one of them into second-last place! This would suggest that they were totally unfit and almost certainly lead to their demise on the Irish team.

## McGann the man
Barry McGann was one of the great Irish rugby fly-halfs and a great soccer player. He was also a little 'calorifically challenged'. Around the time he was first capped for Ireland, he moved from Cork to Dublin and was persuaded to play for

Shelbourne. They had some tremendous players at the time, like Ben Hannigan and Eric Barber. Barry always got a great slagging whenever he went back to play in Cork. One time they were playing Cork Celtic. As he ran onto the pitch, he heard a voice saying on the terraces: 'Who's that fella?'

'That's McGann, the rugby player.'

'Oh, wouldn't you know it by his stomach!'

An even more damning indictment of McGann's bulk was subsequently provided by Tony O'Reilly's quip, 'Twice around Barry McGann and you qualify as a bona fide traveller!'

The battle of the bulge

One of Barry's great expressions was, 'He has two speeds – slow and very slow.'

## Top of the props

Another Irish rugby legend was prop forward Phil O'Callaghan.

Like Moss Keane, Phil O'Callaghan was one of the great characters of the game. He toured three times with Irish parties, to Australia in 1967, to Argentina in 1970 and to New Zealand and Fiji in 1976. Apart from his fire on the pitch, he was also noted for his quick wit. The most oft-quoted story about him is the one about the day a referee penalised him and said, 'You're boring [the term used to describe the way a prop forward drives in at an illegal angle into an opposing prop forward], O'Callaghan.'

Philo's instinctive retort was: 'Well, you're not so entertaining yourself, ref.' The referee penalised him a further ten yards.

During another match, O'Callaghan put out his shoulder. The former Irish captain and leading gynaecologist Karl Mullen attended him. Dr Mullen said, 'I'll put it back, but I warn you it will be painful.' He did and it was. According to the story Philo was screaming his head off with the pain. The doctor turned to him and said, 'You should be ashamed of yourself. I was with a 16-year-old girl this morning in the Rotunda as she gave birth and there was not even a word of complaint from her.'

Philo replied, 'I wonder what she bloody well would have said if you tried putting the f\*\*kin' thing back in.'

One of the highlights of his career was when, in 1967, Ireland became the first team from the northern hemisphere to beat Australia. The Irish party stopped off in Hawaii. At one stage they were standing at the side of a swimming-pool. Philo had his back to the deep end and was pushed in by Mick Doyle. Philo was not able to swim and went under. The guys thought he was faking it when he didn't surface. Terry Moore dived in and lifted him out of the water long enough to give him the air he needed before he went down again. The late Jerry Walsh found the pole for cleaning the pool and extended it to Philo and eventually he hauled himself out of the pool. He asked Jerry later why he had not dived in. Walsh replied, 'Why ruin the tour by having both of us drown?'

### Brothers in arms
One of the giants of Irish rugby is Ray McLoughlin. Ray's brother Phelim also played for Ireland. Phelim modestly said, 'We have 41 caps between us.' What he neglected to point out was that he had only one and Ray held the remaining forty!

### Tom and Noisy
Tom Kiernan was a great motivator. He coached Munster to their win over the All Blacks in 1978, and Ireland to their Triple Crown win in 1982. Before Munster played Australia in 1967, the team met in the Metropole Hotel. Noel 'Noisy' Murphy limped in before the match and said, 'My leg's shagged and I can't play.' A sub was duly called for and informed of his selection. Then Kiernan cut loose with his motivational speech. Everyone was ready to tear into the Aussies afterwards. Noel Murphy was so caught up by Kiernan's emotion that he said, 'Ara, f**k it, Tom, I'll play.'

### Big Tom
No one had a greater passion for rugby in Limerick than Tom Clifford. He was first capped for Ireland against France in 1949, was a key part of the Triple Crown victory in that season, and toured with the Lions to New Zealand in 1950. His name lives on through Tom Clifford Park, a ground which has been variously described as 'The Killing Fields', 'The Garden of Get Somebody' and 'Jurassic Park'.

At Tom's funeral, the church was teeming with rugby folk. The priest giving the homily had been a lifelong friend of Tom's and told the congregation how he had invited the giant of Irish rugby to his ordination Mass. After the ceremony, he asked Tom what he thought of it. Tom replied, 'You spoke too long. The next time, if you go on for longer than ten minutes, I'll set off an alarm clock in the church.' The next Sunday the priest saw Tom arriving in at the church and noticed he had a bulge in his overcoat. When Tom caught his eye, he pulled out an alarm clock.

## The Life of O'Reilly

In the annals of Irish rugby, a special place is reserved for Tony O'Reilly. O'Reilly is very much the Roy of the Rovers of Irish rugby. Having first been capped against France as an 18 year old in 1955, he was the undisputed star of the Lions tour to South Africa in the same year.

As a schoolboy, he also excelled at soccer, playing for Home Farm, but he turned his back on the game following an assault. During a match he made a bone-crunching tackle on an opponent. The boy's mother rushed onto the pitch and attacked O'Reilly with her umbrella. The future Lions sensation remarked, 'Rugby is fair enough – you only have your opponent to deal with. Soccer you can keep, if it involves having to deal with your opponent and his mother.'

Belvedere College provided a nursery for both O'Reilly's rugby and entrepreneurial skills. When he was seven, he was the only boy in his class to make Holy Communion. To mark the occasion a priest gave him an orange – an enormous luxury during the war years. Like most of his friends, O'Reilly had never seen an orange. O'Reilly subsequently claimed, 'After I ate the centre, I sold the peel for one penny per piece, thereby showing a propensity for commercial deception which has not left me since.'

In 1963, following Ireland's 24–5 defeat at the hands of the French, O'Reilly was dropped for the only time in his career. Although the news came as a shock, O'Reilly had arguably never consistently reproduced his Lions form in the green jersey. It seemed after twenty-eight caps his international career was over. Seven years later, in an ill-judged move, the Irish selectors persuaded him to come out of retirement to play against England at Twickenham in place of the injured Billy Brown for his twenty-ninth cap. To put it most kindly, O'Reilly, now firmly established as a commercial giant because of his work with the Heinz Corporation, was anything but a lean, mean machine at that time. His shape prompted Willie John McBride to remark, 'Well, Tony, in my view your best attacking move tomorrow might be to shake your jowls at them.'

Ireland lost 9–3 and O'Reilly gave an undistinguished performance. In the final moments, he dived boldly into the heart of the English pack. As he regained consciousness, he heard an Irish voice shouting, 'And while you're at it, why don't ya kick his f**kin' chauffeur too!' The Heinz slogan is 'Beans Means Heinz'. After the match, a wag was heard to say, 'I never realised Heinz means has-beens.'

## Glory days

One of the giants of Irish rugby in the golden era of Jackie Kyle was Noel Henderson. In the course of a radio commentary on an Ireland international, Henderson was being slated by the commentator. Noel's father was so outraged at the stream of insults that he threw the radio out of the window!

Henderson's most famous pronouncement was, 'The state of British sport is mostly serious, but never hopeless. The state of Irish sport is usually hopeless, but never serious.'

Another of Kyle's teammates was Des O'Brien, who went on to become Irish captain. Before an international, the President of Ireland, Sean T. O'Kelly, the first Irish president to attend a rugby international, was being introduced to the teams. He was a man who was, let's say, small in stature. The match was being played in October, so the grass was long. As captain, Des was introduced to him first. He said, 'God bless you, Des. I hope you have a good game.' Then O'Brien heard a booming voice from the crowd: 'Hey, Des, would you ever get the grass cut so we'd bloody well be able to see the President!'

## I'll do anything for love

One of Des's teammates on the Grand Slam-winning side was J.C. Daly. Jack was an extraordinary character and one of rugby's great romantics. Before the Second World War he only played with the thirds for London Irish. As he departed for combat, he said, 'When I come back, I'll be picked for Ireland.' He was stationed in Italy during the war and had to carry heavy wireless equipment on his back. As a result his upper body strength was incredible. Before internationals he did double somersaults to confirm his fitness. Having scored the winning try to give Ireland the Grand Slam in 1948, he was nearly killed by spectators at the final whistle. His jersey was stripped off his back and people were wearing pieces of it on their lapels for weeks afterwards. Jack was whisked off from the train station in Dublin the next day by a girl in a sports car whom he had never met but who was sporting a piece of his jersey on her blouse. He stayed with her for a week and lost his job when he went back to London!

## That'll Clinch it

In the 1920s, one of the great characters of Irish rugby was Dr Jammie Clinch. When he was a medical student at Trinity College, Dublin, he was sitting on the rail outside when an American tourist emerged from her first visit to the College and spoke to him. 'It's a big place, I've been three hours going through it,' she said. Jammie replied, 'Ma'am, I've been here for seven years and I'm not through it yet!'

# FIVE

# Out of South Africa

**Q: Which was the best ever side to leave New Zealand?**
**A: The 1937 Springboks.**

If Hollywood had been commissioned to write a script for the 1995 World Cup they wouldn't have been able to come up with the fairy-tale ending that saw Nelson Mandela's rainbow nation upset the favourites on their World Cup debut, leaving the All Blacks to blame food poisoning. Sport is more than just mere games. When Mandela walked out to shake hands with the players of South Africa and New Zealand in the moments before the 1995 World Cup final, it was a reminder of how powerful sport can be in symbolising friendship and reconciliation in a public forum. As he presented the trophy to François Pienaar, Mandela wore a replica of Pienaar's number

6 jersey. Here was a man who had spent 27 years in a white man's jail, at a time when rugby had been the tuning fork which the white majority struck in order to conduct the whole orchestra of supremacy, but in his first public appearance supporting what in South Africa had traditionally been a white man's game he chose to wear this white player's jersey. To witness him walk out there and shake hands with the black player Chester Williams and all the white players in the Springbok team bore eloquent testimony to sport's power to heal.

One night, after captaining South Africa to victory, Pienaar was waiting for the bus, not realising that the last one had gone. A driver was on his way back to the garage with an empty bus when he spotted Pienaar and, although it was against all regulations, he stopped and asked him where he was going. When Pienaar told him, the driver said, 'Hop in.' Four miles later the poor driver nearly had a stroke when he saw an inspector standing in the middle of the road waving him down. The inspector was a seething mass of anger and demanded an explanation. 'I have François Pienaar here,' answered the driver meekly.

'François Pienaar? You can't be serious!' said the inspector, boarding the bus to verify the fact. When he saw the evidence with his own eyes, he turned angrily to the driver again.

'How could you be so stupid? Turn around and get back to the garage straight away. How could you drive him in just a single-decker bus? Get him a double-decker straight away so that he can go upstairs if he fancies a cigarette.'

Another joke told about Pienaar goes back to the time he went to his doctor and said, 'I've got a terrible pain in my right arm, doctor.'

The doctor replied, 'Don't worry, it's just old age.'

Pienaar said, 'But in that case why doesn't my left arm hurt too? I've had it just as long.'

# Out of South Africa

## Lights out

On 3 June 1995, in their final Pool A clash in the World Cup, South Africa faced Canada in Port Elizabeth, traditionally a jinxed venue for the Springboks in an evening game. The South African captain François Pienaar noticed how psyched up the Canadians were and how they were talking about going to war, when the lights went out just as the game was due to begin, plunging the ground into total darkness. In the shocked silence that followed, Pienaar heard a Canadian voice calmly saying, 'It's a bit dark, isn't it?'

## Brains or beauty?

The great scrum-half Joost van der Westhuizen managed the seemingly impossible during the 1995 World Cup – he flattened Jonah Lomu in the tackle.

He struck up a remarkable partnership with the gifted out-half Joel Stransky, who is guaranteed to hold a place in South Africa's rugby annals forever because of his thirty-metre drop-goal with seven minutes remaining that won the 1995 World Cup in the 15–12 defeat of New Zealand. At a reception afterwards, Stransky was chatted up by a lady of mature years. Later on, van der Westhuizen asked him what he thought of her. Stransky replied, 'I like a woman with a ponytail, but not when it's hanging off her chin.'

His scrum-half prompted him further: 'Maybe she had brains rather than beauty.'

Stransky replied, 'Not likely! I asked her what her IQ was and she answered "38–34–36".'

## Gone but not forgotten

The late, great coach Kitch Christie steered South Africa to their World Cup victory in 1995 with inspired decisions like sensationally switching Mark Andrews, one of the world's greatest lock forwards, to play at number 8 in both the semi-final and final, despite his complete lack of experience in that position. Before the tournament Christie recalled his experiences as coach of the Transvaal team. A full-back who had dropped a few easy balls and conceded four soft tries was blaming his poor display on ill health.

'I'm not well,' he said. 'I think I must have caught a cold.'

'Thank God you're able to catch something,' came Christie's reply.

He also spoke of a prop forward who walked into a supermarket with a basket and proceeded to place in it one sausage, one rasher of bacon, one egg, one onion, one tomato and then went to the checkout. The checkout girl ran the items through the till and said, 'You're not married, are you?'

The man replied, 'You're correct, I'm single. How did you guess?'

''Cos you're the ugliest man I ever saw.'

He also spoke of meeting a Transvaal fan who told him that he was walking through a graveyard and came across a headstone that read, 'Here lies a journalist, a true and honest man.' Christie said to him, 'Wasn't it strange that they buried two people in the one grave?'

After South Africa's victory in the tournament, at the end of a very long dinner at which there had been too many speeches, the master of ceremonies called upon Christie as the guest of honour to 'give his address'. Kitch rose hastily to his feet and said, 'Ladies and gentlemen, I am delighted to give you my address, which is number 14, West End Street, to which I hope quickly to return.' He then sat down. At first there was a stunned silence, followed by sustained and loud applause.

Another time Christie was addressing a coaching seminar when he was interrupted by a cry of 'Rubbish!' from the back of the lecture theatre. Unruffled, Kitch looked at his accuser with sympathetic concern. He cleared his throat meaningfully before replying, 'We'll take up your special interest in a moment, sir.'

# Out of South Africa

## Style shock

Christie recognised that the Springboks had to stop Jonah Lomu to win that final, particularly as Lomu had played human skittles with England defenders and scored four tries in the All Blacks' 45–29 victory in the semi-final. They did stop him, though, gang-tackling with wing James Small and the peerless centre Japie Mulder leading the way.

Mulder was at the height of his fame after the tournament. A young neighbour, who was six at the time, wanted his autograph. He arrived reasonably early, before Japie went out, and he had been psyching himself up to get the autograph for weeks. He was obviously expecting his hero to arrive at the door wearing a jersey, togs and boots with a rugby ball under his arm because when Mulder appeared all the boy could blurt out, in a tone of absolute shock, was 'You wear clothes.'

## A change of tactics

As hosts of the 1995 World Cup, South African national pride was running very high, particularly when the home nation qualified to meet the mighty All Blacks. Such was the fervour that was behind the national team that there was a sign in a bar which read, 'No All Blacks supporters served in this establishment.' One day a man draped in the Kiwi colours came into the bar. 'I know you don't serve New Zealand supporters, but I'm desperate for a drink and I'll pay 20 rand for a beer.'

The barman thought this over, then decided to serve the drink. It was gulped down in one go. 'Same again,' said the All Blacks fan, 'in fact, I'll have two,' and he slapped 40 rand down on the bar. After a few minutes, he asked for another. The barman said tentatively, 'That's another 20 rand?'

'That's OK,' he said, pushing a 1,000 rand note across the bar, 'I'll have a couple for the road. Keep the change.'

When the drinker had gone the barman put up a new sign: 'Only All Blacks fans served here.'

Come back soon

### Gracious in victory

After the World Cup final loss to South Africa, the All Blacks were making the journey from the stadium to their team bus when they were accosted by two rowdy South African fans. The supporters greeted them with a riddle: 'What do the All Blacks have in common with a wonderbra?'

Without giving the Kiwis the chance to think of a reply, they supplied the answer: 'Lots of support but no cup.'

### Superlative performance

Braam van Straaten is one of the highest Springbok points scorers in the history of the game. He accumulated 221 points in 21 Tests. When asked about his colleagues' performances in a training session, van Straaten once said: 'That was extraordinary. Unfortunately it was extraordinarily bad.'

# Out of South Africa

## Head on

Flanker Joe van Niekerk made his debut for South Africa in 2001 against the All Blacks. When he scored his first Test try against Samoa at Loftus, he threw down the ball in excitement, hitting a Samoan on the head. The captain, Semo Sititi, was not impressed and he took a swing at him. After the game, a Samoan fan said to Joe, 'It's a pity you didn't take up the game sooner.'

'You mean I'd be better now?'

'No, you would have given up long ago.'

## Don't know much about geography

South African fly-half Louis Koen is noted for his intelligence on and off the field. He was amused during the 2003 World Cup to hear one of his teammates responding to a warning about the dangers posed by the Eastern Brown Snake by asking, 'What colour is it?' At another stage during the tournament he heard his colleague asking, 'Is Tasmania an independent country?'

## Name recognition

Rudolf Straeuli was a World Cup-winner with South Africa as a squad member in 1995 before becoming the ninth Springbok coach since they returned from their enforced isolation in 1992. At the time it was suggested that they had more trainers than horse-racing magnate Sheikh Mohammed.

Straeuli had problems replicating his success as a player in his role in a tracksuit. He was a bit nervous one day after his team had sustained a bad defeat when he had to make a public appearance at a rugby dinner. His nerves were calmed immediately when an old man came to greet him and gave him a big smile and most enthusiastic handshake and said, 'It's a great, great pleasure to finally meet you in the flesh. You are a true icon of the game . . . what's your name again?'

Straeuli was an inevitable casualty after South Africa's inglorious exit from the 2003 World Cup. There was much mirth when details of Straeuli's unconventional training methods emerged after the tournament. His idea of building team morale and hunger consisted of getting security guards to force his players down foxholes before dousing them repeatedly with cold water. A new riddle was born:

Q: Why did Rudolf Straeuli turn up to the fancy-dress party dressed as a pumpkin?

A: He hoped he would turn into a coach at midnight.

It is alleged that part of Straeuli's regime in the infamous Kamp Staaldraad (Camp Barbed Wire) involved having the Springboks train in the nude. In fact, so widespread were the allegations that they were training 'military-style' that the National Defence Force spokesman Major-General Mohato Mofokeng felt obliged to state publicly, 'I would like to point out that the South African National Defence Force does not train its people naked, nor, to the best of my knowledge, does any other military organisation. Conditions in the field are not conducive to the naked human form.'

## Those magnificent men in their flying machine

Gary Teichmann is one of South Africa's recent great players. As he was heading off on the plane to play Australia, just before take-off the stewardess asked him if he would like cotton wool or a boiled sweet to combat the pressure differential. 'I'll have the cotton wool,' joked Teichmann. 'I tried the boiled sweets last time but they just kept falling out of my ears.'

## In the Nick of time

Nick Mallett vacated the hot seat as South African rugby coach in 2000. During his tenure he noticed some of his squad lustily scanning two busty blondes in a hotel lobby on the eve of a Test match. Knowing that some of the lads had an eye for the ladies and not wanting them distracted from their rugby he said, 'The only thing that I want to see you trying to pull this weekend is your weight.'

# Out of South Africa

According to folklore, during Mallett's stewardship of the South African team, a fringe member of the squad missed a number of training sessions. Mallett tried to make contact with him but with no success. He had to resort to leaving him messages in all kinds of strange locations. A few days later he got a message on his answering machine. 'Nick, this is X. I'm sorry I missed the last four training sessions. My reasons were compelling and indescribable.' So ended the message, and his brief and undistinguished career as a Springboks player.

## Status symbol

As was the case in most countries, there were some teething problems in South Africa with the transition from amateurism to professionalism. Three Springboks players were in the physio room before a game and were discussing the company cars that they wanted to hire.

The first player said, 'I want a BMW 3 Series.'

The second player responded, 'I'm going for a Rover myself.'

The physio turned to the third player and said, 'I think you need a cortisone injection.'

The third player replied, 'No way, I want a Rover too.'

At the time, graffiti on a wall near Ellis Park read:

Q: What's new about the big South African softie?

A: He's getting paid for playing rugby.

## The end is nigh

In 1994, Ian McIntosh was replaced as South African coach by Kitch Christie. One of the stories told about McIntosh is that he was having a chat with a player who realised he was coming to the twilight of his career, but the end was coming faster than he appreciated. He was speaking to McIntosh about tactics: 'I'm confused, I don't know whether I'm coming or going.'

'My friend,' McIntosh replied, 'I can help you there, you're going.'

## Dead-eye Dick

Such is the fellowship of sport that you would go to war with friends you would trust with your life. That's the theory and often the reality. But not always.

Naas Botha was one of the most prodigious goal-kickers of all time. Hence his nickname 'Dead-eye Dick' – a reputation enhanced by his performances against the Lions in 1980. However, he attracted a lot of controversy in South Africa because of his apparent reluctance to pass the ball.

Botha was playing in a club match during a downpour. His team were on top all through the game and Botha was kicking everything. His right winger was going mad for a pass and eventually Botha gave him one but the winger dropped it and the opposition broke right up to the other end of the field. Botha screamed out, 'That's the last time I'm passing to you until you can drop it further than I can kick it.'

After he kicked his club side's 24 points to give them victory in the cup final, he was sitting beside another man on the plane. Botha was a bit surprised that his companion said nothing to him. After half an hour of total silence, he turned around and said, 'I don't think you realise who I am, I'm probably the most famous rugby player in South Africa.'

His companion quietly said, 'I don't think you realise who I am. I play for your team. I'm your first centre.'

After an injury to his arm, Botha was telling a teammate that he had asked his doctor, 'And when my right arm is quite better, will I be able to pass the ball?'

The doctor replied, 'Most certainly – you should be able to pass with ease.'

His teammate replied, 'That's a miracle cure – you could never pass it before!'

Like many great players, Botha inspired extreme emotions. Even at the height of his fame, he had his critics in South Africa. A fan approached him in the street one day and said,

'Botha, you're the worst fly-half I've ever seen. Why don't you take up snooker?'

Botha's club coach was walking along the street one day carrying a camcorder. He met a fan who asked him what it was for.

'I got it for Naas Botha,' was the reply.

The fan smiled and said, 'Sounds like a damned good swap to me!'

## Straight from the heart

Gysie Pienaar was an immense talent but sadly the international masses never really saw it because of South Africa's isolation in the rugby world. He was the man of the series in the 1980 Lions tour. He had a dream game in each of the four Tests. Everything they kicked at him, he gobbled up. Such was his enthusiasm for victory that in the final Test he asked the referee, 'What's left, ref?'

The referee replied, 'It's over now.'

Pienaar said indignantly, 'Well, blow your f**king whistle now!'

## Mighty Morné

Tempers in the First Test in that series had also become frayed. The most controversial incident in the game occurred at the back of the lineout when Derek Quinnell, of the famous Llanelli club in Wales, hit his opposite number Morné du Plessis an almighty thump and gave him a huge black eye; an incident which, of course, the South African media highlighted and broke down frame by frame on the following day. Some time afterwards, the Lions went to Morné's factory, where he was branch manager for Adidas in Capetown, and naturally he dished out freebies in the hope that the Lions would wear them around South Africa and get good publicity for the sports company. Morné was still modelling a black eye. When the Lions squad entered there was a ripple of polite but lukewarm applause from the factory workers. Quinnell, 'DQ', came in a few minutes afterwards. Immediately the staff nearly lifted the roof with their cheering and applause. Here was the man who had clocked their boss!

Morné was once asked what he thought about an up-and-coming player, spoken of as the next big thing. Morné furrowed his brow and said, 'Oh, he's got a bit of skill. The only problem is that he thinks "tackle" is something you take with you when you go fishing. A good defender should be so mean that if he owned the Atlantic Ocean he wouldn't give you a wave.'

## Danie boy

Any selection of the world's greatest centres must give serious consideration to the claims of Danie Gerber. At the height of his fame in the 1980s, Danie was asked to explain the importance of rugby to South African people. To illustrate, he told the story of the stalwarts of a club in Cape Town who were distraught. One said, 'Have you heard the bad news? Old Frank is dead. And to think he was going to play scrum-half for the Junior B team tomorrow.'

'My God. That's awful.'

'It's tragic! But wait a minute . . . Maybe we can get Joe to fill in for him.'

## Saint Louis

A sport played by men and women with odd-shaped balls is bound to produce moments of mischief and mirth and great characters – and Louis Moolman was one of the greatest. He was seemingly as wide as he was tall and had curly hair and a big beard which made him look awesome; he was sometimes compared to a big grizzly bear. He had a great ability to win the ball at two in the lineout.

Against the Lions in 1980, he was a regular target to receive the ball in the lineout. The only problem was that he was occasionally thrown by the calls. In the Second Test in Bloemfontein, there was a lineout to his team on the halfway line. South Africa had come up with a coded system for the calls to confuse the Lions. The hooker held the ball high and barked out, 'Cape Town, Port Elizabeth, Pretoria, 2, 4, 6, 8.' As the Lions forwards frantically wondered who the ball was going to be aimed at, Louis exclaimed loudly, 'Oops, me again.'

In the Third Test, Bill Beaumont was upset about a South African put-in and said, 'That ball wasn't straight.'

'It was straight as a die,' Moolman replied.

'But it went in between their second row and back row.'

'Fair enough. But at least it went in straight!'

## Coach

Theuns Stofberg was a typical Springboks wing-forward, big and powerful and virtually impossible to get the ball from. He complimented Rob Louw perfectly.

Stofberg was not a big fan of coaches who were strong on theory but weak on practice and results. To emphasise his point, he tells the story of the little boy who came home from school one day after trying out for the junior XV. His father asked him what position he was going to play in.

'I'm not playing in any position,' said the youngster.

'Why not?' asked his father in surprise.

'Well,' said the lad, 'they found out I couldn't run, or tackle, or pass. All I could do was shout and yell. So they made me coach.'

## Rob rule

From time to time Rob Louw would complain to referees. The story is told that, after a series of bad decisions from one ref, Rob approached him and said, 'If I called you a stupid old goat who didn't know the first thing about rugby, what would you do?'

'I would report you and you would be in front of the rugby authorities,' said the ref.

'What if I didn't say it, just thought it?'

'Well, nothing could be done about it.'

'OK,' said Rob, 'we'll just leave it at that, then.'

## Might is right

The 1969–70 Springboks forwards were a massive bunch. When they played Swansea and Martin van Rensberg was injured, the crowd were stunned when they saw his massive replacement, Mof Myburgh. One wag in the crowd shouted, 'Hey, you're only allowed one replacement at a time, not two!'

Forward play is like a funeral. You have to get in front with the family, not behind with the friends. At one stage there was a bit of an altercation on the tour when an opponent was 'putting himself about'. Myburgh told his colleagues to relax because he would look after it. Sure enough, in the second half it was noticeable that the player in question was as meek as a mouse. After the game, when his colleagues asked Mof about the resolution of the incident, he is reputed to have replied, 'I gave him a black eye!'

Another joke told about Mof goes back to the same tour and a match played on a bitterly cold November day. He was being lifted by one of the forwards in the lineout when he shouted down, 'Let me down. My hands are frozen.'

One of the stars on the tour was flanker Jan Ellis. Ellis went to visit a hospital and was told that there was a club flanker receiving treatment the day after a big match.

Ellis asked, 'Did someone make a late tackle on you?'

The club player replied, 'You could call it a late tackle, I suppose. He knocked me down in the bar after the game.'

The side was captained by H.O. de Villiers, their full-back: rock-solid in the bread-and-butter defensive chores, but loved by fans for his all-consuming desire to attack from the deep. He was very modest about his abilities. When the Springboks arrived in Britain, a journalist asked him if he was really as good as everyone said he was. He joked, 'On my day,

I'm the best player in the world. Unfortunately my day is always a Monday.'

## Beauty and the beasts

The 1960–61 Springboks had great forwards. When they beat the Glasgow–Edinburgh XV in Glasgow by 16–11, their front row lifted one side of their opponents' front row clean off the ground. Yet their two prop forwards, Fanie Kuhn and Piet du Toit, got a hard time, particularly from their backs. The standing joke in rugby is 'Prop forwards don't get Valentine's cards for religious reasons – God made them ugly!'

In the international against Scotland at Murrayfield, Abie Malan, the South African hooker, won seven strikes against the head, mainly because of the massive shove generated by the huge South African forwards. One Scottish fan was disconsolate when he heard Malan giving a coded signal before a throw-in from the lineout, shouting: 'Nineteen twenty six.'

'Jesus,' the supporter said, 'they're ordering the champagne already.'

Abie was tickled by a letter written to him by a friend when he won his first cap. The letter read, 'Abie, I should like to impress on you that I'm spending a whole week's wages on travelling to see you play and I beseech you not to make an idiot of yourself on this occasion.'

## A league of their own

It is universally accepted that the 1951–52 Springboks were one of the greatest teams of all time. Their Test pack is the stuff of legend: Geffin, Delport, Koch, Dinkelmann, du Rand, Van Wyk, Muller and Fry. They were huge men who could run and handle the ball like backs. They were very serious and had no time for sentiment, as was evident when they crushed Scotland 44–0 at Murrayfield. As the South Africans walked off the pitch, they heard one of the Scottish fans saying, '44–0! That was dreadful.'

Another responded, 'Och, we were lucky to get the nil.'

The Scots had a good indication of what lay in store for them before the match. Legend has it that the dressing-room was being renovated at the time and there was a six-inch gap in the wall which allowed the visiting side to listen in on the Springboks' team talk. Their captain was exhorting the team to beat these 'haggis-eating pansies'. His concluding remark, much to the mirth of the Scottish players, was 'I'll finish with just two words for you' – there was a pregnant pause – 'A Tack!'

The joke afterwards was that the Springboks were so fired up, when the referee ran onto the pitch, three of them tackled him!

Another apocryphal incident which set the tone for the proceedings was that when the Scottish coach was making his way to the dressing-room he saw a man, who seemed to be about 7 ft tall and the same width, wearing a black beret, approaching him with a menacing look. In a strong South African accent, the stranger barked out at him, 'Are you the Scottish coach?'

The coach knew instinctively that it was not one of those times when honesty is the best policy and said, 'No. I'm their coach driver.'

While they were on that tour, the Springboks found themselves attending the funeral of an ex-Scotland international who was also a decorated soldier. There was a huge crowd outside as well as inside the church. The carriage came out with the coffin draped in the flag, with a hat and a stick on it. The troops sounded the death march and everybody was very solemn. One of the Springboks whispered to his colleagues, 'I see he only got one cap.'

The combination of heavy drinking and the search for romance was to the fore on the tour when the squad heard a rumour one night that there were a number of pretty Scottish nurses locked up in a local hostel. After closing time, they climbed over the walled gate and crept stealthily up to the windows. Just when they reached their vantage point, a large matron came to the window and they beat a hasty retreat. They decided to wait outside until she went to bed, only to discover that she had rung the police. They were introduced to the Scottish accent in all its glory when a big guard said to them, 'Well, ma wee laddies, wha' d'ye think ye're doin' here at this hour o' the nicht?'

'I'm sorry, sir, we got lost.'

'Listen, ma wee laddies, we all know 'tis the nurses ye're after, but let me tell ye one thing: ye're making a fierce mistake – they're the ugliest lot you ever saw!'

## Fiercesome

One of South Africa's most remarkable forwards was Frik du Preez of Northern Transvaal. He lived by the dictum that a forward's usefulness to his side is in inverse proportion to the square of his distance from the ball. He toured the British Isles and France four times, initially as a flanker and later as a lock, and is said to have once drop-kicked a penalty goal 85 yards at the Loftus Versfeld stadium in Pretoria. During a tour to England, he was waiting for a taxi outside a hotel on a poorly lit street. A tiny, timid Englishman looked up at him and asked, 'Did you ever kill anybody?'

Frik shook his head, but before the little man could relax he added, 'Not so far.'

Frik was a tough man who marked tighter than Kylie Minogue's famous hotpants, though the joke goes that when he made his debut for the Springboks, his mother was concerned about the physical nature of the exchanges. She turned to her husband and said, 'Poor Frik will break a leg.'

According to folklore, her husband looked at her reproachfully and said, 'He might, but it won't be his own.'

Another joke told about Frik goes that he had a terrible leg on him, returning to the dressing-room, after a bruising encounter in a Test match. It was covered in cuts and bruises, and had a massive gash from the top of the thigh to the knee. He had no idea whose it was.

Frik's toughness was emphasised in the suggestion from one of his teammates that when he died the words on his tombstone would read, 'What the f**k are you looking at?'

## Blind man's bluff

In the 1950s, the Springboks had an ace place-kicker. Nothing unusual about that, but what was unusual was that he was their prop forward, Aaron 'Okey' Geffin, who was so prolific that he was known as 'the Boot'. Legend has it that after a game when the referee cost the Springboks the match because of a catalogue of poor decisions, Okey approached the referee and said, 'Hi, ref, how's your dog?'

The ref is said to have replied, 'What do you mean? I don't have a dog.'

Okey responded, 'That's strange. You're the first blind man I've ever met that doesn't have a guide dog!'

His fellow prop on the team was Chris Koch, a sheep farmer, who once practised his scrummaging against a stanchion of the stand at Cardiff and made it shake. During that tour to Wales, Koch overheard a row between two members of a club in Cardiff. The secretary was concerned about warped priorities: 60 players had been on a weekend tour of Amsterdam for a Sevens tournament, which they were ignominiously dumped out of in the first round, one short week after they had failed to drum up 15 players to play a team 20 miles down the road. A member of the touring party to Amsterdam responded to the official's criticism: 'Well, to the best of my knowledge, there are no ladies of the night 20 miles south of Cardiff.'

## Some mother's son

The late Hendrik 'Hennie' Scholtz Vosloo Muller was known as 'the Windhond [greyhound] of the Veld' because of his incredible speed. It was also suggested that his nickname should be 'Tow Truck' because he was always on his way to a breakdown. He was one of the top players in the world in the late 1940s and early 1950s. The big number 8, though, was the victim of a practical joke before making his debut for the Springboks. He was desperate to become one of the lads. At dinner, team captain Basil Kenyon asked Hennie to go up to Ernst Dinkelmann and ask him what size shoes his mother wore. Hennie was a bit suspicious but eventually agreed to do so. As soon as he did, Ernst turned away, put his hand over his face and started to sob. Hennie didn't know what to make of this and asked some of the other players what the matter was. They replied, 'Did you not know? His mother was in a horrific car crash a fortnight ago and had both her feet amputated.' Hennie's face turned a whiter shade of pale, and a number of times that night he tried to apologise to Ernst, but every time he got near him some of the players headed him off. The result was it was well into the night before Hennie found out that it was all a con job and he had fallen for it hook, line and sinker.

Hennie had a reputation for getting tough when the occasion demanded it. In a game against a club side in Wales, he was standing on the wing when the opposing winger came charging towards him, but to Hennie's astonishment the player lamely tapped the ball into touch. Hennie asked him, 'Are you afraid of me?'

'No, but I'm afraid of running into your mouth!' he replied.

Hennie once exhorted his side during the half-time talk, 'Now listen, guys, I'm not happy with our tackling. We're hurting them but they keep getting up.'

Asked about his devotion to the game, Hennie joked, 'In my time I've had my knee put out, broken my collar bone, had my nose smashed, a rib broken, lost a few teeth, and smashed my ankle; but as soon as I get a bit of bad luck, I'm going to quit the game.'

One of Hennie's clearest memories about winning his first cap was of a piece written about him in a local newspaper. The journalist in question had rung his mother a few times but had been unable to contact Hennie himself. Yet when Hennie opened the paper he saw a big piece full of quotes attributed to him. Hennie tackled the journalist about this afterwards. He said, 'It's the sort of thing you would have said.'

He didn't have that problem with one newspaper, though. In their case, the difficulty was that he never should have been picked for South Africa in the first place!

Hennie and a friend attended a seminar on coaching in Pretoria one evening, in a school hall run by a religious order. The priest in charge approached the great man apologetically and said, 'There are very bad acoustics here.'

Hennie's friend replied reassuringly, 'Don't worry, Father. I'm not sure who these acoustics are, but if they start any trouble we'll throw them out.'

## Mr Rugby

For years, rugby's most famous official was the late Danie Craven. He was 'Mr Rugby' in South Africa. As South African Rugby Board president, he cast his long shadow on virtually every aspect of rugby. The following story is an ode to his influence and his longevity.

Two elderly Americans were finally discovered and, against all odds, found to be alive in a disused Japanese POW camp, having been captured during the Second World War. They first asked, 'How is President Roosevelt?'

'Oh, he died a long time ago.'

'And how is Stalin?'

'Oh, he died a long time ago.'

'Please tell us that Winston Churchill is still alive and well.'

'Alas, I'm afraid he died as well.'

'Tell us, is Danie Craven still Mr Rugby in South Africa?'

In 1990, a variation on the story came when Nelson Mandela was freed from his years in captivity. The first thing he allegedly said after he was released was, 'Has anyone replaced Danie Craven as the most important man in South Africa since I was thrown into that bloody place?'

## Out of South Africa

Danie was guest speaker at a function. He felt it had gone well and preened himself when he overheard one jovial member saying to a colleague that it had been a very memorable evening. 'Yes,' agreed the second, 'I haven't enjoyed such a good steak for a very long time.'

At another function, Craven was introduced to a family who had a young son. He asked, 'How old are you, little boy?'

'I'm not old,' replied the child, 'I'm nearly new!'

## Tuff stuff

Man is a fighting animal and rugby is a civilised (almost always, anyway) blood sport. Physical exchanges have always been at the heart of South African rugby, which is why it is sometimes said that many of their players like to get their retaliation in first. A correspondent to the *Cape Argus* on a match between the military and civilians in Capetown in 1862 wrote:

> They stamped upon me where I lay,
> How could I rise and kick away?
> Methought, this is but gruesome play!
> A dozen fellows on me lay.
> They almost crushed me into clay.

Bill Beaumont attended a club match on the Lions tour to South Africa in 1980. He was a bit taken aback by the ferocity of the physical exchanges. Asked for a comment, he replied, 'It's not a referee these people need; it's a missionary.'

There's a story told about two grasshoppers who came onto the field before a match as the intimidation started between the players on either team. One said to the other, 'We're going to be killed here today. Do you feel the tension?'

The other replied, 'I do. Hop up here on the ball. It's the only place we'll be safe.'

## Jungle book

With the dismantling of apartheid, Chester Williams was able to play for South Africa in the 1995 World Cup. Injury delayed his participation in the tournament, but he announced his arrival in bold print when he scored four tries in the quarter-final against Western Samoa.

Chester once told the story of a very different match when asked for a funny rugby story. It was the jungle's rugby Classic of the year, the annual grudge match between animals and insects, and by half-time the elephants, zebras and cheetahs had proved too much for the grasshoppers, beetles and ants, with an emphatic score of 63 points to nil. However, when the match resumed, the animals noted that a substitute player ran onto the field with the insects. It was a shiny black centipede. From then on the centipede became the star of the game, peppering the posts with drop-goals from all angles. Indeed, the animals failed to score again and the insects ran out winners, 69 points to 63.

At the bar afterwards the animals' captain, a teak-tough elephant, said to the insects' skipper, a gentle grasshopper, 'Great game, but you were damned lucky that centipede arrived at half-time.'

'You're so wrong,' said the grasshopper. 'He was here from the start of the game, but it took him until half-time to put his boots on!'

## Tougher than the rest

South African rugby players like to keep their friends close and their enemies closer. They take their physical exchanges seriously there. It has been said that one club, who shall remain nameless, have adopted as their own the motto, 'Kick anything that moves above the grass and if it doesn't move kick it anyway.'

The toughest South African club match ever was in 1935. After a penalty kick on six minutes, the ball ricocheted off the post and went into the stand. The physical exchanges continued relentlessly and it was 22 minutes before any of the players noticed the ball was missing!

## Weighty matters

A club in the New Brighton township engaged the services of a massive 280-lb prop forward whose only drawback was that he was rather slow. At a match one Saturday afternoon, this monster was standing motionless in the middle of the pitch, apparently in a trance. 'Van Heerden!' the coach shouted from the touchline. 'Move around a bit! You're killing the grass!'

## Territorial possession

The team captain of the Methodist Rugby Football Club was visiting Pretoria for a match. Walking along the street, he was shocked to see a young girl, about 16 years old, lounging on a street corner, wearing a very short miniskirt, a see-through top, fishnet stockings, and high heels. He walked up to her and said, 'Young lady, what would your mother say if she saw you here like this?'

'She'd be hopping mad,' said the girl. 'I'm on her corner.'

## Trust me. He's a doctor.

Teacher in Cape Town: I thought you told me you wouldn't be in school yesterday because you had to see your doctor?

Pupil: That's right.

Teacher: Then how come I saw you at the rugby match with a tall man in a suit?

Pupil: That was my doctor.

## Downsizing

After the dismantling of the apartheid regime, there were huge changes right across South Africa. One rugby team had been going rapidly downhill, and hit dire financial straits. The club manager came home one evening and said to his wife, 'I think you'd better learn how to cook, my dear, because we're going to have to get rid of the cook. And you'd better learn to clean the house, because we'll have to get rid of the cleaning lady.'

'OK,' said his wife, 'but you'd better learn to make love so we can fire the chauffeur too.'

## Some mothers do have them

Unusually for a rugby player, a scrum-half from Transvaal was completely innocent and on his wedding day he asked his mother for advice. 'Well, son,' said his mother, 'you simply put your . . . you know . . . the hardest part of yourself into her . . . into the place where she wee-wees.' At the honeymoon hotel that night, they had to call for an ambulance. The scrum-half had got his head stuck in a chamber pot.

## Always look on the bright side of life

A player in Bloemfontein always saw the best in every situation, no matter how bad. One day he announced to his teammates that he was going to be married. 'Who's the lucky girl?' asked his captain.

'Amanda Spreadherlegs,' he said proudly.

'You're going to marry Amanda Spreadherlegs?' said the captain. 'She's been laid by everybody in Bloemfontein!'

'Well,' said the new fiancé, 'Bloemfontein's not that big a place.'

## Tender hands

'How are you feeling?' the team captain asked his number 8 sympathetically just before they played a big match against the Proteas in the Dr Craven Stadium at Stellenbosch.

'Not too good, Skipper,' said the forward. 'I've still got this awful sore throat – can't seem to get rid of it.'

'I had the same problem a few weeks ago,' said the captain. 'Know how I got rid of it? Don't laugh – it really worked. I just got my wife to give me a blow job and it cleared up in no time! Why don't you try the same thing?'

'I'll do that,' said the number 8. 'Do you think your wife will be at home this evening?'

## What becomes of the broken-hearted?
A club team were meeting for a cup of tea before a match in the local pub. 'Why are you looking so glum, Kobus?' asked the landlord.

'My wife ran off with my best friend last night,' replied Kobus.

'Oh, no,' said the landlord, 'that's bad news.'

'You're not wrong,' said Kobus, 'he was meant to be playing scrum-half today.'

## A grave matter
On Currie Cup final day, the fans were approaching Ellis Park when a funeral procession went past. Seeing this, one man took his hat off and stood motionless for a moment before walking on. 'That was a nice thing to do,' said his friend.

'Well,' said the man, 'she was a good wife to me.'

## One moment in time
A so-called rugby widow was having a go at her husband. 'Your whole life is rugby,' she moaned. 'You never take me out, you never buy me presents. You're either at a match or watching one on the telly. I bet you can't even remember when our wedding anniversary is.'

'Yes, I can,' replied the husband, 'it's 24 June, the same date that South Africa beat the All Blacks to win the World Cup.'

# SIX

# Men in Black

### Divine assistance

In New Zealand, rugby is like a religion, touching a deep nerve in the psyche of the people of the country. It is recognised worldwide as arguably the spiritual home of rugby. David Thomas famously wrote, 'In New Zealand, if the prime minister died and he had played for the All Blacks, the headline in the papers would be "All Black Dies".' One of the stories often told to demonstrate their love of rugby goes back to 2003 when New Zealand beat world champions and old rivals Australia at a soggy Eden Park to claim the Bledisloe Cup for the first time since 1998. When a fishing boat was devoured in the flames of a bonfire that heralded the success, a sympathiser who offered his condolences to the owner met with an unexpected reply: 'You can buy a boat any time, but not the Bledisloe Cup.'

## Odd-Shaped Balls

An Irish exile living in Wellington had bet a small fortune on long odds for Australia to win. The man explained afterwards that his family had a history when it came to predictions. He elaborated that one of his clearest memories as a child was of his grandad telling him about travelling from Dublin to Belfast in 1911, when it was like going to the moon because of the poor state of communications. They visited the shipyard and read a notice on one of them which stated: 'Even God can't sink this ship.' It was the *Titanic*!

Proof that rugby is the real religion in New Zealand came when Kiwi coaching guru John J. Stewart issued the following prayer to his players:

> Amen, I say unto you that whosoever shall pass the ball under conditions more advantageous to the opposition than his own team will be cast aside.
>
> Verily let it always be that our defence will be desperate and those who set up second-phase play behind the forwards will feel the wrath of the Almighty.
>
> May we always remember to concentrate not on winning but on not losing.
>
> It shall come to pass that the ball will be kept ahead of the forwards, and in doing so may we always remember it can be done by passing or kicking, and kicking is simple.
>
> And as we consider these and other faults, let us be mindful that he who adopts the involved dog position in the rucks shall be smote with a bucketful of water.
>
> From these sins and the national selectors may the Lord protect us.
>
> Dominus tackle, Dominus tackle, Dominus tackle.

## Men in Black

### No ordinary Joe

With the illness of Jonah Lomu, the thrilling Joe Rokocoko's arcing runs became even more important to New Zealand in the run-up to the 2003 World Cup. His value to the All Blacks is reflected in the story of the two fans who were settling down to the Kiwis' opening Pool D match against Italy at the Telstra Dome, Melbourne, when one realised he had left his wallet in his friend's Mercedes. He returned from the car park ten minutes later, pale and shaken.

'I've got bad news, Jim. A lorry's crashed into your Merc and the impact set it on fire. It's totally destroyed.'

'And I have some bad news for you,' said Jim. 'Joe Rokocoko is out injured.'

### Doctor's diagnosis

As a player, John Mitchell lived in the shadow of Buck Shelford and Zinzan Brooke, but when he succeeded Wayne Smith as All Blacks coach his hour had come. Mitchell was a serious man engaged in serious business; he had no time for sentiment and was critical about the tendency in New Zealand to live in the past. An All Blacks fan told a story stressing Mitchell's no-nonsense attitude. One evening he approached a sad-looking fringe member of his panel and asked, 'Why are you looking so down-hearted?'

'The doctor says I can't play rugby.'

'When did he see you play?'

After New Zealand's disappointing showing in the World Cup in 2003, when they lost to old rivals Australia in the semi-finals, Mitchell's New Zealand team was the butt of many jokes:

Q: What's the difference between the All Blacks and a tea bag?

A: The tea bag stays in the cup longer.

Q: What's the difference between an arsonist and the All Blacks?

A: An arsonist never loses his last match.

Q: Why doesn't Joe Rokocoko need any pre-tour travel injections?

A: Because he never catches anything.

## The ageing process

In training camp before the 2003 World Cup, the All Blacks were frustrated that they had to spend so long waiting for their dinner to be served in a posh restaurant. When the meal finally arrived, out-half Carlos Spencer said, 'You tell me you're the same fellow who took my order. Somehow I expected a much older waiter.'

## Born again Christian

In 2003, prior to the Rugby World Cup, New Zealand rugby saw a debate that divided the country like never before. Christian Cullen was widely regarded as the best full-back in world rugby until John Mitchell was appointed New Zealand coach in the autumn of 2001. From the beginning it was clear that Mitchell didn't rate Cullen, and he kept him on the margins. With 46 tries in 58 Tests, as New Zealand's top try-scorer of all time, top try-scorer in Tri-Nations history, top try-scorer in Super 12 history, most capped All Black full-back of all time, 'Cully' clearly had a strong case. In full flight, he lit up the pitch like a streak of forked lightning, flashing brilliantly, thrilling and, from the opposition's point of view, frightening.

Two jokes about selection policy and the New Zealand team emerged. The first involved two men at the bar discussing the big questions of life.

'I'm going to play full-back for the New Zealand team this season!'

'But you don't play rugby.'

'Well, what's that got to do with it? My credentials are impeccable. OK, I've never played at full-back before and OK,

I've never even played rugby before, but more importantly my name's not Christian Cullen.'

The second joke, surprisingly, involved two men at the bar: 'How do the New Zealand selectors pick their full-back?'

'They pick the best man for the job. Hang on, that can't be right. I don't know.'

'They go to the telephone directory, tear out the Cs and stick a pin in one of the pages.'

The Internet carried the lyrics of a song which resonated deeply with many All Black rugby fans entitled: 'Don't Pick Cully'. The lyrics were not number-one material but they had a ring of outlandish truth to them:

> You can pick Joe
> With the broken toe,
> But don't pick Cully.
> You can pick Steve McQueen
> Or any human being,
> But don't pick Cully.

### Aren't you . . .?

Another rugby legend who was controversially left out of the New Zealand World Cup squad in 2003 was the prodigious kicker Andrew Mehrtens. A story told about the former All Blacks fly-half is that one day he was in the supermarket when he saw an old woman looking at him for a long time. He knew instinctively that she was trying to remember where she had seen his face. Finally, she got up the courage to go over and speak to him. He beamed at her and prepared to sign his autograph. 'It is you, isn't it?' she asked.

'Indeed it is.'

'Good. When are you coming back to finish that tiling in my bathroom?'

Despite his sublime skills, Mehrtens was able to handle contact. However, perhaps one commentator created a somewhat misleading impression when he said, 'Andrew Mehrtens loves it when Daryl Gibson comes inside of him.'

## Thunder down under

In the run-up to the 2003 World Cup, many All Blacks were having difficulty accepting the verdict of experts who predicted that England would win the tournament. To redress the balance, they told two stories about Clive Woodward.

In the middle of the night, Woodward was woken up by a call from his local police station. 'I'm afraid the trophy room has been broken into, sir.'

Horrified, Woodward asked, 'Did the thieves get the cups?' 'No, sir,' replied the policewoman, 'they didn't go into the kitchen.'

One day Woodward was walking along a beach when he came across a bottle. When he unscrewed the top, a genie appeared and the genie said, 'I'm so grateful to get out of that bottle that I will grant you one wish.' Woodward thought for a moment and said, 'I have always dreamed that there could be a motorway all the way from outside my front door to Twickenham.' The genie thought for a moment and then said, 'I'm sorry, I can't do that. Just think of all the bureaucracy and red tape involved and all the local authorities who would have to be involved in putting that together. I'm sorry, but could you ask for an easier wish?'

Clive said, 'Well, there is one other thing. I'd like to coach England to win the World Cup.'

The genie thought about it for a few minutes and then said, 'So, do you want two lanes or four on that motorway?'

## Puncturing pomposity

Before New Zealand lost the World Cup semi-final to France in 1999, flanker Josh Kronfeld was in pole position to be named player of the tournament. A few months later Josh attended a rugby reception. Many of the giants of the game like

## Men in Black

Justin Marshall, Andrew Mehrtens, Taine Randell, John Hart, Byron Kelleher, Laurie Mains, Zinzan Brooke and Graeme Bachop were there. An old player, who had the reputation of being an utter bore and whose opinion of his own extraordinary abilities was shared only by himself, approached Josh, looked around the room and said, 'How many great players do you think there are in this room?'

'One less than you think,' Josh replied.

### Knock, knock, knocking on heaven's door

The 1995 World Cup was Jonah Lomu's tournament. The 19 year old who weighed 22 stone but who could run the 100 metres in 11 seconds and score tries at will took the rugby world by storm. Lomu makes every rugby pitch he graces a theatre of dreams, dwarfing all who trail in his wake as he scythes through the defence. In full flight, his hand-off gesture is like a royal dismissal to bewildered opponents reduced to looking like oxen on an ice rink. He enjoys to the full the drama and poetic presence that makes him such a towering presence in recent rugby history. Rugby has never seen a more thrilling sight than Lomu, like a salmon leaping, sailing in a great arc through the air and scoring a try in the corner with a split second to spare.

According to rugby legend, a great Welsh out-half was called to a premature death. He was met at the gates of heaven by St Peter. St Peter apologised profusely for bringing the rugby player to his eternal reward at such a young age but explained that the celestial rugby cup final was taking place and as the manager of one of the teams he needed a star player. The out-half was whisked immediately to the stadium and marvelled at the facilities. They were literally out of this world. Such was the excitement of the occasion that the recently deceased forgot about his death and played the game of his eternal life. With just two minutes to go, St Peter's side were leading by nineteen points when the giant Welshman noticed an athletic sub coming on to the opposition side and, in an accent that was immediately identifiable as Kiwi, giving instructions to his side. The new arrival got the ball four times and scored four tries, each more stunning than the other. He did not bother with the conversions, but had the game restarted immediately – and his team won by a point.

After the game, St Peter rushed on to console his dejected star player. The ex-Welsh player asked, 'Tell me, when did Jonah Lomu die?'

'That's not Jonah Lomu. That's God. He just thinks he's Jonah Lomu!'

## A lapse in standards

It is said that when a prominent former All Black (who shall remain nameless because of the libel laws) dies, the presiding clergyman will have to break with liturgical convention. Such is his liking for publicity that instead of saying, 'May perpetual light shine upon him', the vicar will probably say 'May perpetual limelight shine upon him'. At the opposite end of the spectrum in the modesty stakes is Lomu. He shows the same discomfort with generous compliments that the Pope would be expected to show in a brothel.

He is definitely not the source of a story that is often told about him to highlight what the All Blacks think about England. The All Blacks were playing the English and, after the half-time whistle blew, they found they were ahead 70–0, Jonah Lomu having scored 10 tries. The rest of the team decided to head for the pub instead of playing the second half, leaving Lomu to go out for the second half on his own.

'No worries,' big Jonah told them. 'I'll join you later and tell you what happened.'

After the game Jonah headed for the pub where he told his teammates the final score: 107–3. 'What?' screamed the irate captain. 'How did you let them get 3 points?' Jonah replied apologetically, 'I was sent off with 10 minutes to go.'

# Men in Black

## That sinking feeling

The All Blacks fans can give their own team a hard time on those very rare occasions when they sustain an unexpected defeat. In the 1999 World Cup semi-final against France, they led 24–10 in the second half, with the tournament's top try-scorer Jonah Lomu scoring 2 tries and Andrew Mehrtens in excellent kicking form. Between the 46th and 59th minutes, in one of the most prolific scoring bursts in rugby history, France scored 26 points. The All Blacks lost 31–43, with Jeff Wilson scoring a consolation try in the 80th minute. Some of the All Blacks fans were able to joke that France were the greatest magicians of all time because they made the Kiwis disappear for 13 minutes. A new joke was born:

Q: Why aren't the All Blacks team allowed to own a dog?

A: Because they can't hold on to a lead.

## The Osbornes

The All Blacks full-back in the 1995 World Cup was Glen 'Os' Osborne. Os was not the conventional All Black. On the day of a Test match against France in 1995, Os wanted to get some sleep before the match. The team doctor carefully instructed him that he should only take half a sleeping tablet. Os, though, was not into half measures and took two of them. He had to be carried into the changing-room before the match. When he was eventually woken up, he promptly walked straight into the big mirror, thinking it was another changing-room. There was a row of bottles of all kinds of energy drinks laid out on the table. One bottle on the table was clearly labelled 'massage oil' and all the bottles for drinking were bright red. For reasons nobody could ever understand, Os decided to take up the massage oil and drink the full bottle. The French had never faced such a slippery customer. He played the game of his life, catching every high ball in sight and scoring a hat-trick of tries.

One evening, a few of the All Blacks players invited

themselves to dinner at Glen's house. After the meal, Os said he was going to have a bath. His guests told him they would do the washing-up. The problem was they couldn't find the washing-up liquid. The kitchen was searched high and low, and eventually Jonah Lomu was delegated to go into the bathroom to ask Os where it was. When Lomu walked in there were bubbles all over the room. When he asked where the washing-up liquid was, Os replied, 'Mate, it's here,' and he plucked it out from under all the bubbles.

'What's it doing in the bath?'

'Well, I needed some bubbles for my bubble bath.'

## Fired with enthusiasm

Professionalism raised the standard of rugby around the world after it was officially introduced in 1995. The downside was that there was no longer any room for sentiment. Inevitably there had to be casualties. A former All Blacks panellist, who must remain nameless, stormed into the coach's office and raged, 'If the manager doesn't take back what he just said to me, I'm leaving the club!'

'What did he say?' asked the amazed coach.

'He said, "You're fired"!'

## Get an earful of this

Asked for her opinion about rugby, Elizabeth Taylor replied, 'It seems a neat game, but do they really bite ears off?'

South Africa's Johan le Roux bit Sean Fitzpatrick on the ear, tearing flesh, in the 1994 series in New Zealand, and was sent home in disgrace and banned for 19 months from international rugby. Afterwards, the New Zealand media joked, 'Fitzy's fine but le Roux's in hospital with blood poisoning.'

When Fitzpatrick was fired up, everybody knew the All Blacks were in a mean mood. In 1995, in a pool game in the World Cup, they defeated Japan 145–17 in a 21-try extravaganza. The mistake the Japanese made was scoring a try.

If they hadn't had the cheek to score a try, the All Blacks would have let them off with a 50-point defeat. During half-time, the Japanese captain was asked to say a few encouraging words to his team. All he could say by way of tactical insight was: 'We're going to retreat carefully.'

According to legend, when Fitzpatrick was asked what Japan needed to do to become a power in world rugby, he replied, 'The manager needs a new Chinese assistant: "Winonesoon"!'

Mind you, Fitzpatrick has been the subject of the odd cutting remark himself, notably when a journalist claimed that, after exhaustive research, he could reject the malicious rumour that when Fitzpatrick was a child, he was so ugly that they had to tie a lamb chop around his neck so that his dog would play with him. The journalist was so emphatic because he had proved conclusively that Sean never had a dog.

## Number two to the number 2

Warren Gatland was in the right place at the wrong time. He established himself as the number two All Blacks hooker. The only problem was that Sean Fitzpatrick was the number one at the time!

As a coach, Gatland had more opportunities to shine. Before retiring from Wasps in 2005 and returning to New Zealand he brought Wasps to the summit of English and European rugby, Gatland was in charge of Ireland. Peter 'the Claw' Clohessy sometimes had problems deciphering Gatland's Kiwi accent. On tour to Australia, the Claw was having trouble sleeping and Gatland suggested he take a sleeping pill before the Second Test. The morning of the game Gatland asked the Claw how he had slept. He replied, 'Great.'

'Did you take a pill?' asked Gatland.

The Claw looked very sheepish as he replied, 'Yeah, yeah, I did.'

'Did you get one off the doc?'

'What?'

'Did you get a sleeping pill off the doc?'

'Aw, f**k, is that what you meant? I thought you'd asked me if I'd had a pull, not a pill.'

Gatland also tells the story of how one day Trevor Brennan came to him in training and said he was feeling a bit tired, and wondered if he had any suggestions. Gatland replied, 'Take four or five bananas and that should help.' The next morning Trevor went up to apologise profusely: 'Gats, I'm sorry, I could only manage twenty-nine bananas.' Gatland shook his head as he said, 'Trevor, I said four or five bananas, not forty-five!'

## Wife wanted

In 1987, the All Blacks reached the inaugural Rugby World Cup final. The country went into a dizzy state and tickets for the match were chased with a passion. An advertisement appeared in a magazine in Wellington a few days before the final: 'Young rugby supporter of good appearance and sound health offers hand in marriage to any young lady with two tickets to the World Cup final. Please send photograph of the tickets.'

The All Blacks' dominance ensured a bleak time for their old rivals Australia. This was most obvious on the side of a bridge in a town in a remote part of Australia where a sign read, 'You are now entering a Nuclear Free Zone'; a Kiwi fan added a message of his own when he visited the town a few weeks after the final: 'You've now entered a Trophy Free Zone.'

## An Englishman abroad

John Gallagher was the only Englishman to win the World Cup before 2003. He played full-back for the All Blacks in 1987. He was born in London and didn't go to New Zealand until he was 20. The Monday after the final, he was back at work as a policeman.

At one stage John was invited to attend a major corporate event on the theme of motivation. He sat at the back of the conference hall while the opening speaker gave a most boring speech. Halfway through it he noticed his distinguished guest and said, 'If you can't hear me at the back, there is a vacant seat at the front.'

Gallagher replied, 'I can't hear you, but I'm quite happy where I am, thank you.'

## Friendly advice

Murray Mexted had many of the traditional strengths of an All Black number 8 but was not your typical dour forward. He was a colourful personality and a talented player, very slim with a big knee lift, and very hard to knock off the ball. He could play the ball wide or mix it up front. His personality is probably best summed up in a conversation he had with his former teammate, Jamie Salmon. Salmon made history by becoming the first player to be capped for England having previously been capped for New Zealand. In a quirk of fate, Salmon's England debut was against the All Blacks. Mexted rang Salmon to wish him well and arrange to meet for a drink afterwards. All was sweetness and light until they were exchanging goodbyes, when Mexted said: 'Oh, by the way, Jamie, if you come back on the switch during the game, I'll take your f\*\*king head off!'

## Time, gentlemen, please

The acclaimed coach Wayne Smith moved to Italy in 1986 to coach a club called Casale sul Sile. His job required him to work closely with the team manager, Dino Menegazzi. Dino was a little gullible, so easy meat for a wind-up. Smith's new club were going to Rome to play the local team. Smith went into a coffee shop with Menegazzi and started reminiscing about life in New Zealand. Dino was trying to come to grips with the 12-hour time difference and asked, 'What time would it be in New Zealand now?'

Smith replied, 'Well, it would be about one o'clock tomorrow morning.'

'Nah, it can't be tomorrow down there. Really?'

'Well, if I rang my parents they could tell us if we won the game or not.'

Dino scratched his head, looked at Smith and suddenly slammed his fist on the table and said, 'Ring them, and if we haven't won, we won't play.'

## The haka

For years the All Blacks have tried to intimidate opponents by performing the haka:

> Ka mate! Ka mate!
> Ka Ora! Ka Ora!
> Tenei te tangata puhuruhuru
> Nana nei i tiki mai whakawhiti te ra.
> A upane, ka upane!
> A upane, ka upane
> Whiti te ra!
> (It is death! It is death!
> It is life! It is life!
> This is the hairy person
> Who caused the sun to shine.
> Abreast, keep abreast!
> The rank hold fast
> into the sun that shines!)

No All Blacks game would be complete without it. As a norm, the opposition react by not reacting and feigning indifference. One man, though, was determined to do otherwise.

As Irish captain, Willie Anderson was renowned for a famous piece of sporting theatre before Ireland played the All Blacks in 1989, when he led the Irish team literally up to the noses of the All Blacks in an effort to intimidate them.

Years later, when Ireland played New Zealand in the Bermuda Classic, the Irish players knew Willie would have something special planned for the haka. The New Zealanders were led in the haka by their lady physiotherapist. Willie kept his hands behind his back until they had finished, when he walked up to her and pulled out a big bunch of flowers.

Another time Ireland faced the All Blacks and, as they started the haka, the Irish players theatrically swung over their legs. The All Blacks weren't sure what the Irish were up to until they started singing, 'You put your left leg in, your left leg out . . .' The whole place cracked up.

Put your left leg in . . .

### Wet, wet, wet

On 14 June 1975, the All Blacks lined up against Scotland in a Test match at Auckland. Scotland lost 24–0, but the match is best remembered for taking place on a flooded pitch. Ian McLauchlan famously said after the game, 'It was sheer bloody luck that nobody got drowned.'

Many of the All Blacks had Caledonian ancestry. When asked to comment, Ian McGeechan said of the All Blacks, 'They're just Scots who've got used to winning.'

In New Zealand, though, the Scots are not so highly thought of. In 1990, the All Blacks defeated Scotland 31–16 in the First Test in Dunedin. The *Auckland Star* headline, however, was 'All Blacks Scrape Through to Win Over Scotland'.

Scotland's penchant for the ten-man game on that tour did not endear them to the media in New Zealand. Steve McMorran wrote in *The Dominion*: 'It became an overriding impression that Scotland might have significantly reduced the cost of their tour by leaving behind the greater part of their backs' contingent. They don't use their backs, therefore they don't need them.'

### Pine Tree

Colin Meads was as hard a man as anybody ever came across on a rugby pitch. His brother Stan was also a tough nut. Colin (nicknamed 'Pine Tree') was the best, most aggressive and perhaps the most totally committed player of his generation. Close at hand, he looked like King Kong! A small indication of his rugged indestructibility was his remarkable recovery from a horrific car crash in 1971. His back was in plaster after the accident, but he was playing rugby within six months. The New Zealand legend was not impressed by wimps or poseurs. Meads made a sweeping denunciation of English rugby as comprising 'too many sweatbands, not enough sweat'!

### Grizzly Alex

They don't come much tougher than Alex 'Grizz' Wyllie. The former All Blacks coach was not a man to mess with on the pitch, as Ireland's fly-half Mick Quinn discovered to his cost on Ireland's New Zealand tour in 1976. Ireland were losing 15–3 to Canterbury. Quinn was a sub. From his point of view, everything was going great. When you're a sub, you don't really want things to be going well for the team because if it does, how are you going to get your place back? Full-back

Larry Moloney broke his arm, so Tony Ensor replaced him. Wallace McMaster got injured and with a sinking in his heart Quinn realised he would have to play on the wing. It was his first time ever playing in that position. He was petrified and wished he was wearing brown shorts!

As he walked on, Grizz Wyllie came over to him and said, 'You've come a long way to die, son.' When Quinn was at school, his coach had always drilled into him the belief that he should never let anybody intimidate him and so at this stage he made the biggest mistake of his life. He said to Wyllie, 'Listen, pal, if my dog had a face like yours I would shave his arse and get him to walk backwards.' Every chance Wyllie got after that, he clobbered Quinn. Even when the ball was somewhere else, he kept coming at him. When the Irishman said, 'The ball's over there,' Wyllie answered, 'I couldn't give a f**k where the ball is. I'm going to kill you.'

## A Gray area

The late Ken Gray played for the All Blacks as both a lock and a prop forward in the 1960s. One of Ken's favourite stories was about the club coach in Wellington who burst into the changing-room as the second half of the game was about to begin.

'All right!' he roared. 'All of you lazy, no-good, thick-headed b*****ds – out on that field – now!'

All the players jumped to their feet and rushed out onto the field – except for the full-back sitting in the corner.

'Well?' roared the coach.

'Well!' said the full-back. 'There certainly were a lot of them, weren't there?'

Gray had this trick he sometimes played on a player gaining his first cap. A lot of players, before their debut, start to feel that they are a bit sluggish and not at their best. Ken would pretend to be very sympathetic and tell them he had the solution. He would inform them in the strictest confidence that the top players always took a freezing cold bath to give them an edge in a big match. The only reason why this was not generally known was that it was a trade secret.

He joked that the biggest casualty in all of this was Sid Going. They put him in a cold bath and added buckets of ice. They told him he had to wait in there for 20 minutes, otherwise it was no good. Sid was squealing like a pig. When his time was up, he couldn't move and had ice on his legs. Ken's reaction was simply to say, 'It gives a whole new meaning to the phrase "hard going".'

### Going, going gone

Sid Going was the All Blacks scrum-half for ten years. He exposed the old myth that the New Zealanders and the Welsh are beloved enemies: 'It's just so much heifer dust. The Welsh hate our guts . . . Welsh supporters are one-eyed and Welsh players are cheats . . . You never really beat the Welsh, you merely scored more points than they did.'

### Fast talker

When he was manager of Blackburn, Kenny Dalglish was asked by a journalist for a quick word. Dalglish famously replied, 'Velocity!'

All Blacks prop Keith Murdoch had a more prosaic reaction when a journalist asked him if he could spare a couple of words. Keith replied, 'Sure. F**k off!'

### Frank the flanker

Jack Manchester captained the All Blacks in the 1930s. He never ceased to be amazed that rugby players attracted smart women. Clearly opposites attract. He told the story of a club player in Invercargill, Frank the flanker, who was accosted by a prostitute one evening. She said, 'Hello, darling, shall we get together and have some fun?' 'Sure,' said Frank. He took her round to his place and they spent the evening playing

Monopoly. Not only was Frank dim, he was also lazy. In fact, he was so lazy he got himself engaged to a pregnant woman.

Manchester was a great admirer of the pride people took in playing rugby football for their local side and told a story to illustrate this. Within hours of the tragic death of the scrum-half in a traffic accident, an ambitious young hopeful rang the local club chairman. 'I hope you don't mind me ringing at this time,' he said, 'but I was wondering whether I might take the place of the deceased.'

'I hadn't really thought about it,' replied the chairman, 'but if the undertaker doesn't mind, then neither will I.'

## Reid on

Tori Reid was the only Maori on the New Zealand side that toured Britain and Ireland in 1935–36, and as a big forward he cut an imposing figure. Despite his immense skill, Tori was never too bothered about tactics. Asked by a journalist for the reason for a vintage All Blacks performance he answered: 'We'd decided to go out in the first half to soften them up and kick the proverbial sh*t out of them. And it went so well for us that we had a quick word at half-time and decided to kick the sh*t out of them in the second half!'

## Bob the boot

Bob Scott, the All Blacks full-back in the 1940s and '50s, was known as 'the Barefoot Boy' because he regularly kicked goals in his bare feet from the halfway line. Bob played his club rugby with Auckland. At one stage a disgruntled Auckland player, unhappy that he had not made a first-team appearance in six months, came to Scott and asked, 'Why am I on the second team?'

Scott looked at him sympathetically, shook his head and patted the player on the shoulder before he answered in a whisper, 'Because we don't have a third team.'

## Simply delicious

One man's meat is another's poison. President George W. Bush's favourite food is said to be bull's balls.

The winter solstice on 21 December is a big day for those who lean towards paganism, tree-worship, shamanism, dancing around an oak tree at midnight, chanting and assorted mumbo-jumbo of the non-orthodox variety. For others, it is a time to be spiritually elevated, unlike Bart Simpson, who was asked by his mother, 'What special event do we commemorate at Christmas?'

To which he replied, 'Er . . . the birth of Santa?'

Most people are waiting for the birth of the new day, and a new year vibrating with promise, bringing inescapable excitement to all, with the sense of a new opportunity offered, a fresh beginning possible. In Papua New Guinea, the first rugby club always held its annual dinner on 21 December. The membership was made up almost exclusively of cannibals. There was a special dinner to mark the end of the first captain of the club's year of office. During the course of the meal, one member turned to his neighbour and said, 'You know, I don't really like the captain.'

'Really?' said the neighbour, after a pause pregnant enough to give birth to triplets. 'In that case, why don't you just eat the vegetables?'

## The sun will come out tomorrow

A club team in Auckland had very modest expectations. Their motto was 'We'll get them next time'. One Saturday morning their players were in great form because they believed they were in with a good chance of winning. Then the match started . . .

## Safe sex

A woman in Christchurch believed in responsible sex. She made passionate love during the safe period – when her husband was playing in an away match.

## Men in Black

### Is small beautiful?

An unusually tall scrum-half on Chatham Island fancied himself as a ladies' man. He took his girlfriend to a hotel for a night of illicit pleasure, and they both removed their clothes. She took one look at his tackle and said, 'Just who do you expect to satisfy with that?'

'Me!' he replied.

### Deep throat

A woman in Dunedin bumped into her next-door neighbour and asked: 'How's your husband?'

'He's laid up in bed with a rugby injury.'

'I didn't know he played.'

'He doesn't. He sprained his larynx at the match last Saturday.'

### Contractual difficulties

An undistinguished player in Oban took everyone by surprise when he announced that he was halfway along the road to rugby superstardom. He had just signed a full-time contract to play with the All Blacks. All he needed to do was to persuade the All Blacks to sign it as well.

Another Oban player's dedication wasn't quite as intense. The night of the presentation of the medals, he had a few glasses of wine too many and as he drove home he was unable to take a corner and drove his car through a wall, absolutely wrecking his car in the process. A passer-by was soon on hand and recognised the driver, even though the blood was pumping out of his forehead like Niagara Falls. The player instructed the passer-by to shine his torch into the car. 'Are you looking for your medal?' enquired the good Samaritan.

'No. I'll find that some time, but I've got a big bottle of whisky in here somewhere and I want to be certain it didn't break in the crash.'

## Odd-Shaped Balls

### Love and marriage
A club team outside Auckland were in the dressing-room, one player short. 'Where's Brian?' said the full-back to the captain.

'Oh, apparently he was getting married at half past two,' said the captain.

'Sh*t,' said the full-back, 'that means he won't get here till the second half.'

### The last resort
A young prospective bank official was being interviewed for a job in Wellington. The bank manager was chairman of the local club and said, 'We need a scrum-half with courage and a strong set of hands like yours.'

'Sorry, sir,' said the lad, 'I don't know a thing about rugby.'

'No worries. We need referees too.'

# SEVEN

## Oz-some

### David the Goliath

David Campese was the most swashbuckling of rugby buccaneers. With his goose step, great acceleration, ability to drift around players, phenomenal try-scoring record and desire to run the ball from anywhere, he is unquestionably one of the all-time greats of rugby. He was happiest when the ball was being moved and he was taking risks. Of course, sometimes mistakes happened, like the one which let in the Lions for the try that decided the series in 1989. But for every one he gave away he created another nine, and that's some ratio. Even when the Aussies lost, Campo always played in a style that embodied the old French rugby dictum, '*Ceux qui ne connaissent pas la joie de la victoire, en attaquant, ont toujours le droit de sourir devant l'existence.*' (Those who do not meet with the joy of victory

189

while playing attacking rugby have at least the right to smile in the face of existence.)

His status in the world of rugby is reflected in a question from an Aussie journalist to the management when he was told in 1988 that David Campese was jogging in water in order to ease a groin strain: 'Did you say in the water or on the water?' He was a genius, but so unpredictable that Nick Farr-Jones said of him, 'Sometimes his brain doesn't know what his feet are doing.'

Campese liked to enjoy himself before a match. Simon Poidevin went out for a walk the night before a friendly international and when he came back he saw Campo, all dressed up, with a number of business friends. Simon called over and he said, 'Campo, it's a great thrill for me to see you here.'

'Why's that, Simon?'

'Well, in all the years I've known you, it's the first time I've seen you in the team hotel the night before a match!'

Campo said of himself 'I'm a great off-field sledger' ('sledging' is the art of verbal abuse of an opponent). He loved to slag off players, especially 'Poms' (the English), though he conceded that Martin Johnson was 'a real fair dinkum player'. Campo's description of an English player who had a reputation for being a ladies' man was, 'He thought he was the world's best shagger until he found out that his girlfriend had asthma.' During the 1991 World Cup, Campo was talking with his captain Nick Farr-Jones about one of the English forwards. 'He's so slow it's hard to imagine that on the night he was conceived out of 10,000 sperm he was the quickest.'

In the summer of 1998, Clive Woodward brought an under-strength England team on their 'tour from hell', losing 76–0 against Australia. It is easy to see why Campo was attributed with a comment actually made by an Aussie fan watching England take a hammering in the match who afterwards was asked, 'Were the England team good losers?'

## Oz-some

'Good? They were perfect!'

Campese was not Will Carling's biggest fan: 'Carling himself epitomises England's lack of skills. He has speed and bulk but plays like a castrated bull.'

### On a wing and a prayer

> There he stood, poor little chappie,
> Looking lonely and unhappy . . .
> When a thousand voices screamed a startled 'Oh!'
> I looked up. A try or something?
> Then sat gaping like a dumb thing.
> My children, somebody has passed to Lowe.

P.G. Wodehouse was so shocked when England's winger Cyril Lowe actually got a pass that he wrote this poem. One of England's most famous wingers, Rory Underwood, would have readily understood that centre's frustration, because he seemed to spend much of his international career waiting for a pass. Indeed, it is surprising that he never got the nickname 'Cinderella' because it often seemed nobody wanted to take him to the ball. David Campese, whose own career coincided with the best of England's flying winger (he worked as a pilot), once remarked: 'The only thing you're ever likely to get at the an end of an English back line is chilblains.'

### The price is not right

In the early 1990s, Bath supremo Jack Rowell thought big. Officially, rugby remained one of the great amateur sports until 1995 – though the only real sporting amateurs are those who pay their own expenses. He attracted big names like Simon Geoghegan, who made the journey from London Irish to play with Jack's army. While Simon was a big-name acquisition, Rowell had earlier tried to bring David Campese to Bath from Milan. He got somebody to investigate how much it would cost to get Campese to sign on. When he heard the figure £200,000, he gulped, but immediately did his sums and speculated that over three years it worked out at £67,000 per annum, which just might be possible. The plan was abruptly shelved when Rowell was told that Campo's contract with Milan was not for three years but for five months!

On the field, Campese was unquestionably the greatest entertainer rugby has ever seen. Off the field, he is pretty entertaining too. He was always a man to get the last word. At one stage he was invited to make a lucrative personal appearance at an agricultural show. A sceptical, obese farmer questioned his knowledge of agricultural matters: 'How many toes has a pig got?'

Campo's answer came with lightning speed: 'You take off your boot, mate, and count them.'

Since his marriage in 2003, Campo's macho side is less to the fore. Some of his jokes are even printable! Mind you, he is unlikely to become a pin-up boy for feminists. A typical Campo joke is as follows:

Q: What's Australian for foreplay?

A: Brace yourself, Sheila.

### Positional sense

With the ball in his hands, Campo was a sight to behold, but he was not above passing the buck. In those days you didn't have the organised defences you have now. Normally it was man-to-man marking. Players took up their opposite number. In a game against France, one of their wingers, who was Campo's opposite number, came through like a rocket between Andy Slack and Michael Lynagh and scored a try. Campo came up to Slack afterwards and said, 'He was your man.'

Campo once joked that Lynagh was not a great tackler and if he'd had to play rugby as a forward he would never have played the game! For a warm-up game against a club side before embarking on a tour, Michael Lynagh was surprisingly switched from out-half to centre. As out-half, Lynagh was a scoring machine, amassing a then record 911 points in Test games for Australia, and he was explaining his puzzlement about the selection to David Campese when they were out for a short walk just before the game. The ever helpful Campo told Lynagh that he was delighted he was playing in the centre. Lynagh's morale lifted straight away and he enquired why. Campo said, 'Now at least we'll have somebody at out-half who can make a tackle.'

Campo could be very loquacious at Australian team meetings. At one, captain Nick Farr-Jones concluded, as was his custom, by asking if there were any questions. Campo asked, 'What I would like to know, captain, is is there any way of knowing will the out-half be taking his man for a change?'

Campo paid an interesting tribute to Lynagh after a friendly game. The Australians beat an exhibition side 28–12, with Lynagh giving a virtuoso performance, scoring 24 points including 3 tries. Campo scored the other try to complete the team's scoring. In the dressing-room, Campo turned around to Lynagh and said: 'Wasn't it great that it was only you and I that scored, mate?'

There were times when the roles were reversed. In 1992, Campo was with Michael Lynagh at a festival. It was not long after Australia's World Cup victory and they had a very high profile then. At one point, Campo was conscious of a group of girls looking at them. He heard murmurs of, 'Yes, it is', 'No, it isn't'. Shortly afterwards, he felt someone tap him on the shoulder. It was a young lady who asked him if he was David Campese the rugby player. When Campese said he was, she turned around and went back to her friends. Campo heard her whisper, 'I've never been so disappointed in all my life. He's nowhere near as good-looking in real life as he is on television!'

Lynagh gave rugby a wholesome image. When he went up in a two-seater plane with Campo, the winger shouted, 'If we fly this plane upside down, will we fall out?' Lynagh replied, 'Don't be stupid, we'll still be friends.'

Lynagh tried to stimulate Campo's intellect. He didn't always get the response he was looking for. During a flight from Australia to England, Lynagh decided to play a game with his teammate. 'Some plants have the prefix "dog". For instance, there is the dogrose and the dogwood. Now name another plant prefixed by "dog".' Campo was silent for a long time. Finally he shouted in triumph, 'Collieflower!'

There were times when Campo's taste for joking around did not endear him to Lynagh. Hence the joke:

Q: Why did Michael Lynagh cross the road?

A: To get away from David Campese.

### Straight talking

One day before a club match in Italy, Campo was giving the team talk to boost the team's morale. He put his hand on his fly-half's shoulder and said, 'Claudio, in years to come, rugby people will be sitting around their fires and they'll be talking about the great fly-halfs of all time.' He paused and you could see Claudio's chest swelling with pride. 'And you know something, Claudio? When they do, you won't even get a mention.'

Campo's ability to tell it as it is didn't always have the results he anticipated. He was in a hotel one evening when the venue was descended upon by a party of women. Anxious to find out the nature of the occasion, he asked one if it was a hen party.

'No,' she answered, 'it's a weight watcher's convention.'

'Oh, not been going long?' he enquired casually. That was the moment she floored him with a cracking right hook.

### Smells like?

Hooker Brendan Cannon made his international debut for Australia against the British Lions in 2001. During his career, Cannon has faced some memorable opponents in the front

# Oz-some

row. The strangest one, though, was an opposition tight-head prop who fell on top of him in a club game. He asked Cannon probably the oddest question that has ever been asked in the front row of the scrum: 'That's a nice aftershave you're wearing – what sort is it?'

## Rub-ish

Rugby is a game for hooligans played by gentlemen. One of rugby's great gentlemen is the Australian full-back Matthew Burke. Accordingly, his colleagues were surprised when he was a bit grumpy during the build-up to the 2003 World Cup. Ace place-kicker Elton Flatley asked him what was wrong. Burke replied, 'Ah, nothing, I was just watching a Walt Disney film and I didn't like it. That *Aladdin* rubbed me up the wrong way.'

## Records are meant to be broken

At the 2003 World Cup, Australia chalked up a record score of 142 points against Namibia, including another record of 22 tries. Before the game, the Namibian coach Dave Waterston was asked how he felt about facing the Aussies. He replied, 'I've got a bottle of Johnny Walker Blue which I'm going to consult tonight and come up with a plan.'

The Australian fans' verdict on Namibia's place in the rugby hierarchy is reflected in the following story they told after the match. A young boy's parents were being divorced. The judge asked him, 'Would you like to live with your father?'

'No, he beats me.'

'So you would like to live with your mother?'

'No, she beats me.'

'Well, who would you like to live with?'

'The Namibian rugby team – they can beat nobody!'

## I am sailing

Australia are masters of 'roll-on', i.e. quick-fire, sustained attack with fast-recycled ball. Wallaby runners attack continuously, some as decoys, some as shadow runners, forcing the opposition to defend countless threats. A key player in all of this is their right-winger Wendell Sailor, who regularly knifes through opposing defences. One of the stories told about Wendell is that he was driving to a remote small town to play in a charity match and, after he parked his car, he approached a local man and asked him, "Scuse me, where's the nearest boozer?'

The man replied in a slurred voice, 'You're talking to him.'

## By George, I think he's got it

In the last decade, the traditional springboard for many Australian attacks has been their scrum-half George Cregan. His teammates, though, were never shy of making up stories about him. One told the story of an evening Cregan was propositioned by a lady of the night. She said, 'Would you like to sleep with me for 20 dollars?'

Cregan is said to have replied thoughtfully, 'I'm not very tired, but the money will come in handy.'

## Tall order

There is no finer exponent of the lethal running line than Australia's fly-half, Stephen Larkham. According to folklore, before Australia played England George Cregan said to him, 'Never mind Martin Johnson. Remember – the bigger they are, the harder they fall.'

'Yes, I know that,' said Larkham. 'But what if he falls on me?'

## Lugergate

Before World Cup 2003 the Aussie press were scornful of claims that England would win the competition. They told a story about an incident in darkest Africa where there was a river infested with crocodiles. On the other side there was a tribe which various missionaries wanted to convert. However, nobody was willing to take the risk of crossing the river. In spring 2003, along came a group of missionaries who waded across the river without coming to any harm. Shortly after, they revealed their secret: 'We wore T-shirts bearing the words "England – World Cup Champions 2003". And not even a crocodile was willing to swallow that!'

Another story was that God challenged the Devil to a rugby match. The Devil agreed, provided the match was played in England. 'Remember,' said God, 'we have all the good players up here.'

'Yes,' said the Devil, 'but we've got all the referees down here.'

During World Cup 2003, the Australian media never missed the opportunity to put the boot into the English team. 'Lugergate' afforded them the perfect opportunity. England's Dan Luger came on as a substitute and played against Samoa as a 16th man without another English player leaving the pitch for a brief period before the officials spotted the transgression. The *Sydney Morning Herald* saw the humour in the situation and began its preview of England's next game with a nice little barb: 'Clive Woodward sprang a surprise yesterday by naming only 15 players in his team to meet Uruguay in Brisbane on Sunday.'

However, the most noteworthy piece of Pom-bashing during the tournament came from Australian journalist Mike Gibson. He wrote: 'England, boring? We're talking about a nation of people whose idea of risk-taking is to buy a ticket in the pools. Whose idea of excitement is to join a queue. This is a country where the liveliest sporting action is found under the staircase at Buckingham Palace.'

## Fighting talk

Australia's inspirational number 8, Toutai Kefu, was a tough man to tackle. His colleagues sometimes tried too hard to emulate his example. He was playing a club match and the side was facing defeat. At half-time the coach roared some fight into them. 'And you, Eddie, it's about time you got ferocious.'

'What's his number?' asked Eddie.

Kefu was unwittingly part of one of the great wind-ups of Australian rugby. On his first international tour with the Wallabies, to Italy, Kefu was introduced to the president of the Australian Rugby Union, Phil Harry. The other Wallaby players had all told Mr Harry that 'Tongan Bob', their nickname for Kefu, who was of Tongan extraction, was from a remote Pacific Island village and had only a few words of English. Harry tentatively introduced himself: 'Tou . . . tai, . . . me . . . Phil . . . Harry . . . big . . . chief . . . of . . . Australian . . . Rugby . . . Union. Fly . . . over . . . on . . . big . . . plane . . . to . . . watch . . . you . . . play. You . . . played . . . very . . . well.'

Harry had completely misinterpreted the look of ever growing bemusement on Kefu's face. In actual fact, Kefu had been born and bred in Brisbane and all the squad collapsed with laughter as Kefu replied uncomfortably, 'Gee, thanks, mate.'

Kefu made a memorable foray into Pom-bashing during the 2003 World Cup: 'Go back to history, look at the English army. Who goes to war wearing red coats?'

## A sense of place

The Queensland Reds were on a mini-tour in South Africa. They had played the Stormers and were training in Cape Town. Their next opponents were the Blue Bulls at altitude at a town called Brakpan. A TV journalist came up and asked the Australian full-back Chris Latham for an interview. The request was graciously acceded to.

'How do you think your form is at the moment?'

'Yeah, I'm pretty happy the way things are going. The team's playing well.'

'And a good performance against the Stormers . . .'

'Yeah, we're happy with the way things are progressing,

annoyed to have lost by just a couple of points, but concentrating on the next match.'

'So what do you know about Brakpan?'

'Well, I reckon he has a pretty good step and a tidy mispass . . .'

'Erm, erm . . . actually, erm . . . I'm really sorry, Chris, but can we do that last bit again? Brakpan is actually where you're playing!'

## Perfection personified

The opening line to the fourth film in the Star Wars series was: 'In every generation a new hero is born.' The line could have been written for John Eales. The former Australian captain's nickname is 'Nobody', as in 'nobody's perfect'. Mind you, Eales has often pointed out that nobody has ever called him 'Nobody' to his face.

Just as a girl who is born beautiful can only enhance her looks a little bit, you can only achieve a limited amount in rugby by coaching. It's really a question of natural ability. Eales was gifted with extraordinary levels of natural ability. A powerhouse in the scrum, he was one of the few forwards – like 'the Panther' from Aberavon, Allan Martin, who toured with the Lions to South Africa in 1980 and kicked five penalties and three conversions in his thirty-four appearances for Wales – who was also a very accomplished place-kicker.

In 1996, Eales toured Ireland with Australia. There was one heart-stopping moment for him on the tour. He was having his breakfast at the team hotel in Dublin when a message came over the intercom for Eales to contact reception urgently. The message was repeated two further times in tones of ever increasing urgency. Becoming concerned and suspecting a family crisis at home, he identified himself and was quickly given a telephone.

'Mr Eales.'

'Yes?'

'This is your 8 a.m. wake-up call . . .'

Unlike most rugby players, Eales is renowned for his politeness as much as for his prowess in the second row. In 1999, when the team were checking in to their hotel in Perth, he said to the lift attendant, 'I'd be grateful if you could let me off at the sixth floor – if it isn't out of your way.'

During the Sydney Olympics in 2000, Eales was one of an elite number of Australian personalities who was invited to tour the athletes' village. When he went into the cafeteria, he sought to engage one of the athletes in conversation. In his typical deferential manner, he said: 'I hope you don't mind me asking but are you a pole-vaulter?' The man turned to him and replied, 'No, I'm German, but how did you know my name?'

In a desperate attempt to combat the rugby-watching public's perception of Eales as a semi-godlike figure, some of his former international colleagues have started to make jokes about his abilities at golf. They say his first game was a disaster but his golf slowly improved. Eventually he hit a ball in one! Even at his very best, he always took two or three lumps with his tee. He bashed his way around the course, cutting divots from fairway and greens alike and left a trail of disaster. On his third and final visit, he was approached by a stern-faced official who pompously said, 'I am chairman of the Green Committee . . .'

Eales is supposed to have replied, 'I'm delighted to hear that. In fact, you're just the man I wanted to see. I had lunch in the restaurant. Those Brussels sprouts weren't fresh.'

His 'friends' claim that, such was Eales' desire to find an outlet for his competitive instincts when he retired, he entered a pun contest. He sent in ten different puns in the hope that just one might win. Sadly, no pun in ten did.

After the scars of that experience had healed a little, he made the switch to playing football as a goalkeeper. It quickly emerged that he had a Dracula complex. He had serious problems with crosses.

Of course, none of these stories are true, but there was one memorable time that Eales did face a potential rift with his most illustrious colleague. In 1992, Australia were on tour in Wales. Eales was approached by his prop Ewen McKenzie, who asked him if he had read the autobiography of the Scottish rugby captain, David Sole. Ewen proceeded to show him a passage that immediately drained all the blood from the great man's face: 'There is probably nothing I can say about Campo that he hasn't already said himself . . . as the Wallaby lock John Eales said: "David fell in love with himself ten years ago and has remained faithful ever since!"'

Eales wished the ground would open up and swallow him. He had jocosely mentioned that phrase as one of the Wallabies' favourite lines in the course of a private conversation with Sole. However, he never expected to read it in cold print, with Australia's most iconic figure sitting just a few yards away from him. After the initial fear subsided, Eales decided to deal with the problem head on and broach his indiscretion directly with Campo. He knocked timidly at Campo's door and after some prevarication eventually mustered up the courage to meekly ask, 'Campo . . . have . . . have you . . . have you seen David Sole's new book?'

Much to Eales' relief, Campo replied with typical indifference, 'Naaaah, mate, I wouldn't read something like that if you paid me. Who cares?'

Eales almost danced with joy and said, 'Good. You're not missing much. It's really terrible.'

It was a much relieved Eales who went to bed that night. The following morning, Eales confided his faux pas to prop Tony Daly. Daly told him that all his angst was needless. 'You needn't have bothered speaking to Campo about it in the first place. He couldn't be bothered even reading his own book yet, so there's absolutely no way he would even think about reading David Sole's!'

### Free Willie

One of Eales's most famous teammates was the explosive Willie Ofahengaue (frequently nicknamed 'Often-Has-A-Go' by the Wallabies). One of the stories told about him goes back to early in his career. After sustaining an injury, Willie went to the hospital. An elderly doctor was on duty and was more interested in reading the *Sydney Morning Herald* than attending to Willie. Without looking up from his paper, he asked the player what was wrong. The star said, 'I think I've broken my nose.' With no concern in his voice, the doctor told him to go over to the mirror and clean off the blood. When this task was completed the doctor enquired, 'Does it look different than it did this morning?'

Willie replied, 'Yes, it's crooked.'

The doctor calmly replied, 'You probably broke your nose then.'

### Trivial pursuit?

It's funny the things that go through players' minds during a big game. During the 1991 World Cup quarter-final, Australia's great centre Tim Horan was in a panic. After Gordon Hamilton scored a sensational try to give Ireland the lead in the dying minutes, Tim thought it was all over for them and they would be on the plane home the following morning. He had put a lot of his clothes in the laundry that morning and his big fear was that the clothes wouldn't be ready for the following day! Then Michael Lynagh intervened and took them out of jail with his try.

### I want your sex

In the World Cup final itself that year, Horan had an even more pressing distraction. In the build-up to the final, the Australian team had an amazing amount of support from well-wishers, not just the fans who cheered them on their way but also many who sent messages to the team hotel. In the lead-up to the final, from time to time the players went into the team room in the hotel to read the messages. The messages were incredible: some offered free accommodation at five-star hotels, free evenings at massage parlours, free beach holidays – but then came the classic. A woman from Adelaide had faxed in: 'To whoever scores the first try in the final, I will offer you fantastic free sex.' Then she added her phone number.

Once the game started, the first break in the match happened to come from Horan. He was racing down the right-hand side with only Will Carling between himself and the try-line, with this incredible offer also at stake. Was he about to get lucky twice in the one moment? He decided to chip through but the ball went into touch. From the ensuing lineout the Australians managed to pilfer possession, and the forwards drove over the line. The prop, Tony Daly, crashed over the line to score this crucial try and became an unexpected hero, scoring the only try of the match. Tony was a wonderful old-fashioned prop who won 41 caps for Australia, but he had no future as a male model and was no George Clooney.

As the whole of Australia watched the game on television, the nation's telephone company had its quietest two hours ever. They only took a single call. A lady from Adelaide had rung in to say that she wanted her number changed immediately!

Daly was famous for his impression of John Eales. When Eales became team captain, he was famous for the lengths he would go to in order to reach a consensus. Daly regularly entertained his colleagues on long bus trips by mimicking the way Eales called lineouts: '19, 67, 45, 22 . . . if that's OK with everyone, I mean. Anyone got any thoughts? I'm very happy to change it. Everyone's got to be in agreement with the decision.' Daly also called Eales 'City Ford' because he said 'Yes' more often – their television advertisement used it as its slogan.

Daly was also believed, though it was never proved, to be

responsible for a classic wind-up of David Campese. While the team were staying in a hotel in London, a woman approached Campo in the lobby and said, 'Are you John Eales?'

Campo replied, 'No, I'm not.'

'I'm glad. I wouldn't like to see him looking so bad.'

## The Italian job

In 1992, Tim Horan went to visit his good friend Michael Lynagh in Treviso, Italy. The perfect host, Lynagh was anxious to show his guest a good time, and accordingly he organised a trip to what is regarded as one of the most stunning cities in the world – Venice. When they arrived, Horan did not have the reaction his friend was expecting: 'Bloody hell, it's been raining a lot here, mate, all the roads are flooded.'

'No, Tim, this is what Venice is like, it's made up of canals, that's how you get about, all by water.'

'But, mate, where do all the cars go?'

## Advice column

Tommy Lawton was at the vanguard of the changing role of hooker. He was a huge man who was extremely mobile around the field, with his own unique style. Tommy was also noted for his quick wit. Once, when a young hooker asked him how the ball should best be thrown into the lineout, he replied, 'Low and crooked.'

## R.S.V.P.

One of Sean Fitzpatrick's most ferocious rivals was Australia's Phil Kearns. During a Bledisloe Cup match between Australia and New Zealand, the Wallaby hooker and captain shoved two fingers in Fitzy's face after yet another heated altercation. When asked about the incident, Kearns calmly replied, 'Well, I was just inviting him to a barbecue and I wanted to know if he wanted one sausage or two.'

Kearns's nickname in the Wallaby squad was 'Lightning'.

When he was throwing into the lineout, he never hit the same spot twice.

### It takes two to tango
Personal contests in rugby can generate a lot of fun as well as rivalry. As recently as the 1980s, Australia's Andy Slack and New Zealand's Stu Wilson played a game within a game whenever they played against each other, even in a high-pressure situation like a Test match. Slackie carried three Australian coins in his pocket and Wilson three New Zealand coins. At various stages of the game they dropped a coin from their pockets. The winner was the one who collected the most of the other's coins during the match. The loser bought the drinks. That kind of sideshow doesn't happen today.

### Everybody needs good neighbours
Games between Australia and New Zealand are very keenly contested. The intense rivalry on the pitch is only matched by the rivalry of the fans off it. Before the 1999 World Cup, Australia fans rewrote the Snow White story. In their version, Snow White arrived home one evening to find her house destroyed by fire. She was doubly worried because she'd left all seven dwarfs asleep inside. As she scrambled among the wreckage, frantically calling their names, suddenly she heard the cry, 'New Zealand for the World Cup!'

'Thank goodness,' sobbed Snow White, 'at least Dopey's still alive.'

### Crime and punishment
Australia were playing New Zealand and there was a terrific lightning strike. Tragically, Ewen McKenzie and Buck Shelford died, but before they were allowed into heaven they were sent to purgatory. There Shelford met McKenzie, who was walking along arm in arm with a beautiful young page-three girl.

'Well!' said Shelford, 'I see you're getting your reward up here while you purge your sins.'

'She's not my reward,' said McKenzie. 'I'm her punishment.'

## An age-old problem

In the early 1990s, before Australia played old rivals New Zealand, the squad were relaxing watching television when second-row Garrick Morgan walked in. Pointing to the TV, he asked, 'Who's that?'

'Mikhail Gorbachev.'

'What does he do?'

'He's the leader of the Soviet Union.'

'What's that on his head?'

'It's a birthmark.'

'How long has he had it?'

## Making his mark

Mark Ella was a massive talent with his sleight of hand, deceptive change of pace and adhesive palms. He had amazingly quick hands and they would grab anything in sight, literally like a claw. At one stage, Ella played an exhibition game against a club side for an Australian selection. Their opponents were lucky to keep the defeat down to 60 points. Ella went into the opposition dressing-room afterwards, where the players were in a state of shock at such a hammering. Ella told them not to worry, they would get another chance, and asked the winger how he had got on. He answered, 'I sidestepped you five times. The only problem was that you had the ball each time!'

## A royal performance

Australians have mixed views on the role of the Queen in the state. This is often reflected when Australia play England in the players' different reactions to members of the Royal Family in the pre-match presentation ceremony. One player was keen to establish his royalist credentials. Before the game, they were introduced to the Prince of Wales. As they shook hands, he said to the Prince, 'Everyone at home is asking for you!'

The other debate that divides Australian public opinion is: rugby union or rugby league? Hence millionaire businessman John Singleton's assertion that, 'Anyone who doesn't watch rugby league is not a real person. He's a cow's hoof, an ethnic, senile or comes from Melbourne.'

## Keeping up with the Joneses

In Australian rugby, hard work on the training pitch is a necessity. Former Aussie coach Alan Jones once said, 'I take the Gucci view about hard work on the practice field – long after you have forgotten the price, the quality remains.' Yet for all his obsessive will to win, Jones had a sense of humour. At one stage he was introduced to a multimillionaire entrepreneur. The businessman explained that, although he had earned millions of pounds, been to the most famous places in the world and had a beautiful wife and family, he would give the vast majority of his fortune just to play rugby once for Australia. Sharp as a tack and never lost for a word, Jones replied, 'Well, if you'd just like to slip me a few of your millions, I could probably arrange that for you.'

## Plan B?

Jones coached Australia to new heights on their 1984 tour of Britain by introducing a new concept of back play, with a flat alignment that enabled them to breach the gain-line quickly, and with wonderful pass improvisation as they performed a dazzling repertoire of mis-moves, loops and intrusions, all at high speed with incredible skill levels. Such was his focus on tactical innovation and theory, the joke in the Australian squad about tactics was, 'That will work brilliantly in practice but does it stand up in theory?'

At the end of a weekend squad session, team captain Andy Slack joked to the media that Australia now had a Plan A and a Plan B. Asked to explain what that meant, he said that Plan A was for the Australian side to kick the ball high at the opposition and chase after it. 'And Plan B?' asked a journalist.

'Plan B calls for us to kick it even higher!'

Another player to get in on the act was captain Nick Farr-Jones, who was asked to share his thoughts on tactics. He joked, 'They're cool, minty and sweeten your breath.'

## May I have your attention please

According to legend, Andy McIntyre, former Australian prop, was playing for his club in a key fixture and the match was building up to a tense climax when a message came over the Tannoy: 'Could the owner of car registration number — please move their car.'

Andy was forming a scrum at the time, but he ran to the sideline and admitted that it was his car that was blocking the ambulance. The match was held up for five minutes while he got his keys.

## Come dancing

At fourteen and a half stone, Australia's full-back in the 1980s, Roger Gould, was a formidable figure whether initiating an attack from the deep or augmenting the back line. He was not always the lightest on his feet on the dance floor. At a post-match function, he was dancing with a rather haughty woman, the wife of a prominent official, who was getting somewhat annoyed with his clumsiness. After stepping on her toes for the third time, he said apologetically, 'Please forgive me. I'm a little stiff from rugby.'

'I don't give a damn where you come from,' she replied. 'This is the last time I'm dancing with you.'

# Oz-some

## Believe it or not

Like John Eales, Australia's open-side George Smith is known as one of the more polite players in rugby. His former coach, Rod Macqueen, has experienced another side of Smith's character, though. Before the First Test against the Lions in 2001, Macqueen was driving from Sydney to Canberra and was ringing the players in his squad individually to let them know whether they were selected or not. The phone was on speaker for ease of driving, with his wife in the passenger seat. Smith was just breaking onto the team at the time and, as is normal in these situations, he was being constantly wound up by his teammates with all kinds of phone messages purporting to be from the Australian management. When Macqueen rang Smith to tell him the good news that he had made the team, he was more than a little surprised by Smith's reaction. The conversation unfolded as follows:

'Hi, George, it's Rod Macqueen.'

'Yeah, sure, f**k off.'

'No, George, seriously, it really is Rod Macqueen. Congratulations, you're in.'

'What a load of b*****ks.'

'George, if you don't believe me, please ring any of the other members of the management and check it out.'

Ten minutes later, Macqueen took a call. It was Smith. The aggression had melted and was replaced by deference. 'Mr Macqueen, erm . . . it's George Smith here, Mr Macqueen . . . erm . . . sir, I'm so, so, so sorry . . .'

## Skylab

One of the stars of the 1987 World Cup was Australia's giant second-row Steve Cutler, nicknamed 'Skylab' for obvious reasons. Cutler was guesting on a celebrity team playing in a charity fund-raiser. A diminutive winger attempted to tackle him when he was charging forward with a try in sight. The winger, nicknamed 'Tiny Tim', bounced off Skylab and went crashing to the ground writhing in agony and clutching his private parts. The trainer ran onto the field with his first-aid gear and, as he approached the injured player, who was squirming on the ground with his hands clutched between his legs, the winger moaned, 'Please, don't rub 'em! Just count 'em!'

## Death wish

The Wallabies toured the British Isles in 1948. Things heated up when they played Munster. Munster had a very simple way of dealing with touring sides. This was to bring them down to their level as soon as possible, and then it would be an even match. Nick Shehadie, one of the stars of the Australian side, was confronted by Tom Clifford. Shehadie was a bit taken aback by the opening line, 'Come in here, son. You may as well die here as in f**kin' Sydney.'

After the match, Shehadie was told that one of his opponents was getting married the following day. 'Congratulations, my boy,' said Shehadie. 'I'm sure you'll look back on today as the happiest day of your life.'

'But I'm not getting married until tomorrow,' protested the young player.

'I know,' said Shehadie.

## Chess nuts

A large number of chess enthusiasts had checked into the hotel the Australian team were staying at in London; they were standing in the lobby discussing their recent victories. After a few hours, the manager asked them to disperse. 'But why?' they asked.

'Because,' he said, 'I can't stand chess nuts boasting in an open foyer.'

## High infidelity

A former Australian player would occasionally stray from the marital bed. A journalist once asked, 'Did you have a hard time trying to explain the Test match to your wife?'

The player replied, 'Yes, especially when she found out I wasn't there.'

## Light and darkness

A couple of fans were watching a club match on a particularly dark and dismal afternoon in New South Wales. Neither team was on top form and the match had rapidly become as dull as dishwater. Suddenly the stadium lights flickered and then went out, leaving the pitch in semi-darkness. It was impossible to continue and the match was quickly abandoned. 'Well!' said one fan to his friend. 'That's the first time I've ever known bad play to stop light.'

## Tight fit

A rugby team celebrated their victory in a tournament in Canberra with a night on the town. One of the prop forwards ended up with a lady of the night in her flat. After the act of sexual intimacy, he said, 'I'm sorry, Sheila – if I'd known you were a virgin, I'd have been more gentle.'

'Virgin?' she said. 'You must be joking! If I'd known you were going to be gentle, I'd have taken off my tights.'

## Long distance

A prop forward was driving to Albany for an important match. On the way, he picked up a stunning female hitchhiker, and halfway there, he put his hand on her knee. 'You can go further if you want,' she said softly. So he went to Perth.

## Seeing is believing

A tiny scrum-half joined a big club in Melbourne and found himself dwarfed by the big 200-pounders. Nobody seemed to pay any attention to him and he began to wonder whether he was being deliberately snubbed. He approached the captain and told him of his troubles. The captain smiled sympathetically and said, 'Don't worry about it, son. They're not giving you the cold shoulder. They just haven't seen you yet.'

### Little and Large

Melbourne rugby has always been a place where the weak don't survive. Hence a club secretary's report which stated, 'Frank Mitchell [the name has been changed to protect the guilty] made his debut in such a way that he will never be asked to make it again.'

### Blind as a bat
During an international between Australia and Fiji, the referee found himself being constantly barracked by one particular member of the Australian crowd. When the spectator shouted, 'Oi, ref – that was a foul! Are you blind or something?!', the referee strode over to the stands and said, 'What did you say just then?'

'Blimey!' said the spectator. 'He's not only blind – he's deaf as well!'

### The centre of attention
A paranoid referee suddenly walked off the pitch in the middle of a club match in Sydney. As he explained to his psychiatrist the following day, 'Every time they went into a scrum, I felt they were talking about me.'

### A mother's love
Two young kids in Perth were arguing. 'My father is a better rugby player than your father,' said one.

'Maybe so,' said the other, 'but my mother's better than your mother!'

The first lad said, 'You may be right there. My dad says the same thing.'

### Tender loving care
On a very crowded golf course in Melbourne one day, four women were teeing off and there were four rugby players ahead of them. One of the women hit the ball like a bullet and before she could shout 'fore', it hit the full-back ahead of them. He hit the ground holding his crotch and fell into the foetal position. The ladies were embarrassed when they went over and saw the man writhing on the ground. After they regained

their composure, one of the women said, 'I'm a physiotherapist and I will deal with the problem. Would everyone please leave me alone with this poor man for a few minutes.' Everybody moved away. At first the man refused to let her touch him but eventually he yielded to her feminine charm. She opened his trousers and massaged him gently on the crotch area for five minutes and then tenderly asked, 'How does that feel?' The full-back replied, 'It feels terrific, but my thumb is killing me!'

# EIGHT

# Wish You Were Here

### Trains, boats and planes

A rugby tour has a number of striking similarities with a religious pilgrimage, such as uniformity in dress code, the chanting of familiar songs and a feeling of community and fellowship throughout. The analogy does not hold true for the Wasps tour to Malaysia in 1992, when some of the tourists bared their posteriors for the world to see. Not surprisingly in a Muslim country, this cheeky behaviour caused outrage and the offenders were severely fined and deported.

These trips have a unique capacity to produce tales of the unexpected. In 2002, the Ireland rugby team visited Siberia to play a match in an area renowned for its freezing temperatures. As the players are a very pampered lot, they can normally get everything they need. On this trip, incredibly, they found there was one thing they couldn't get – ice-cubes!

Not every top player is a fan of tours, though. When Welsh international Scott Gibbs was asked to explain why he gave up touring, he replied, 'I don't want to be institutionalised in a hotel, singing stupid songs and showing my arse to all and sundry.'

Lions tours in particular are the stuff of legend – as much for their off-field activities as for all the epic games on the field. For a novice, a Lions tour is a journey into the unknown. One player on the Lions tour to Australia in 2001, who shall remain nameless, was told he would be 'dirt-tracking', a well-known rugby term for not being in the first team on tour. But rather than being downcast, he was excited by the news, declaring that he loved BMXs and asking where the track was! Another was to learn much to his embarrassment that, on tour, when a player expresses an interest in having a 'blowjob', in this context a blowjob means a short.

## Judge and jury

No player on that tour got more media coverage than Austin 'Oz' Healey. Very little of it was for his contribution on the pitch. His abrasive personality guarantees that he gets under the skin of many people, none more so than some of his teammates. Healey had a major disappointment in 2001 when he failed to make it on the Lions starting team for the Test games. His anger was largely directed against the Lions coach, Graham Henry. Shortly after he returned home, Healey bumped into Ian McGeechan, who had coached the Lions to glory on their previous tour. Ian asked, 'Austin, how did the tour go?'

'Oh, terrible, terrible. Henry took an instant dislike to me. An instant dislike.'

'Why did he take an instant dislike to you?'

'I suppose he just wanted to save time.'

After the Lions tour, Healey went into a hi-tech electrical

store to buy a car radio and the salesman said, 'This is the very latest model. It's voice-activated. You just tell it what you want to listen to and the station changes automatically. There's no need to take your hands off the wheel.' On the way home Healey decided to test it. He said, 'classical' and the sound of the BBC orchestra filled the car. He said, 'country' and instantly he was listening to Dolly Parton. Then suddenly a pedestrian stepped off the pavement in front of him, causing Healey to swerve violently and shout at him, 'f**king idiot'. Then the radio changed to a documentary on Graham Henry.

## Snakes alive

On the 2001 Lions tour to Australia, four of the squad, Rob Howley, Derek Quinnell, Dafydd James and Brian O'Driscoll, were at a zoo and were being shown a snake. The snake-handler explained, 'This is a 25-foot Asian python. This type of snake is capable of eating goats, lambs and is reputed to have eaten humans as well.' The four brave Lions were ready to beat a hasty retreat when a photographer who was working with the team came up: 'Right, lads, let's have a picture, all four of you holding the snake! No getting out of it, you're all doing it.'

Realising that they had to have their photo taken, Quinnell immediately rushed forward and grabbed hold of the snake's tail. Howley and O'Driscoll copped on immediately and stepped forward smartly. Dafydd James couldn't fathom why his three friends were suddenly keen to embrace this huge great snake. Then, too late, he twigged what was going on. O'Driscoll and Howley had grabbed the middle section of the snake and there was only one place left for James in the photo. He had to hold the python by its head, all flicking tongue and gleaming eyes. The photo showed three happy Lions and one looking absolutely terrified!

After the tour Jonny Wilkinson described Brian O'Driscoll as 'the Monica Seles of table tennis. You've never heard grunting like it'.

## Murder most foul

In 2001, Harlequins travelled to play Munster in the Heineken Cup. As it was a crunch match and Munster were very difficult to beat at home, the Quins players went to bed early. Two of Quins' English internationals, Will Greenwood, aka Rodney Trotter according to some English fans, and Tony 'Dippers' Diprose, were rooming together. Very early in the morning they were rudely awoken by a loud banging on the door. They assumed it was someone straggling in from a nightclub who didn't know where he was, and didn't respond, but the banging continued. Then a booming voice said, 'This is the police, open up.' The two internationals replied in unison: 'Yeah, yeah, sure, p**s off, will you.'

'Open up immediately, there has been a murder,' said the booming voice.

'Very funny, now p**s off.'

They were convinced it was a wind-up. As the banging persisted, and because of the tone of the man's voice, Dippers eventually got up and opened the door where he was confronted by two massive policemen. 'About time, too,' said one. 'There has been a murder, we would like to question you.'

The rugby stars were immediately freaked out, worrying that one of their teammates might have been killed. The talkative policeman walked into the room and immediately recognised Greenwood, the centre with a phenomenal try strike rate who had twice toured with the Lions: 'Oh, hello, Will, howya doing?' The fact that he was in the middle of a murder hunt was forgotten. For his part, Greenwood was bursting to know the details of the crime and have his anxieties about his teammates placated, but the policeman continued, 'Nice to welcome you to Munster, I'm sure there'll be a warm reception for you at Thomond Park this afternoon. Anyway, the weather's due to be blustery, may be a hint of rain, wasn't it a great result for the Irish, beating you recently?' The two English players were subjected to the policeman's views on every aspect of the game for almost half an hour, but no reference to the murder. They were anxious to get the details and then get back to sleep, and eventually managed to steer the policeman round to the murder. He replied, 'Oh, yes, that murder, it obviously wasn't you two, we know that, but lovely to chat. Oh, and by the way, Munster will win today.'

He was right.

## Hot Rod

Rugby tours can be a good test of the player–coach relationship. When a rift emerges, because they are eating, sleeping (in a sense) and drinking together, it can be like a volcano waiting to explode. When the Australian team were on tour, their coach Rod Macqueen couldn't believe how popular he was with the players when they got to the golf course. Everyone wanted to play a round with him. The players never carried much spending money and knew that when they played with Rod he would feel obliged to pay the green fees. Hence his nickname: the ATM – Automatic Teller Macqueen.

## Discretion is the better part of valour

In 1999, France toured Argentina for the Mar del Plata Sevens. The French were winning in front of over 30,000 passionate home fans. Prominent international referee Chris White was in charge of proceedings. A moat and a fence separated the pitch from the stands but the teams were in range of various fruits thrown by the crowd. The French captain went down injured in range of the crowd. White went to check him but was hit on the calf by a huge orange and had to be treated by a physio. France went on to score a last-minute try to wrap up the match – right in the corner. The kicker walked back for the conversion, right next to the moat, fence and crowd. A barrage of fruit rained down. The terrified French kicker enquired: 'Monsieur l'Arbitre, what are you going to do about this?'

White calmly replied, 'I'm going to stand in the middle of the pitch while you take the conversion.'

## Brothers in arms

In 1997, before the Lions went on tour to play World Champions South Africa, a Cape Town paper carried the headline: 'These Are Not Lions But Pussycats'. The Lions had the last laugh, as they won the series. Key to the success of the tour was the unity of purpose shared by all in the party, players and management, a unity that was missing four years later. The players did some unusual things to keep spirits up on the 1997 tour. Matt Dawson asked Keith Wood for a hair trim; Wood shaved all his hair off.

New nicknames were lavishly doled out. Lawrence Dallaglio was nicknamed 'Lawrence Bowleggio', because you could drive a bus through his legs. Jeremy Davidson's nickname was transformed into 'Buzz Lightyear' because of his jaw, especially as it looks like he's always chewing marbles. Will Greenwood was nicknamed 'Shaggy' because he looks like the character in *Scooby Doo*. Keith Wood became 'the Irish Sperm Whale', or 'Fester', because he looks like Fester from *The Addams Family*.

The Lions kept tabs to ensure that miscreants were punished appropriately for misdemeanours such as poor dress sense. Austin Healey, 'the Gimp' for his transgressions on tour, was stripped to his underpants and had an apple stuck in his mouth and tied to his head with electrical tape in a re-creation of the scene from *Pulp Fiction*.

When a friend rang from England, Will Greenwood took the call and said, 'Austin can't come to the phone. He's a bit tied up at the moment.'

While he was bound, Healey asked if he could go to the toilet. 'Only if you recite the alphabet,' replied Lawrence Dallaglio.

'OK,' said Austin. 'ABCDEFGHIJKLMNOQRSTUVW XYZ.'

'Where's the P?' asked Dallaglio. 'Halfway down my leg,' said Healey.

## Raise your glasses

The night before the First Test in 1993, the Lions were watching the forecast with keener interest than usual. As the weatherman was giving the details, Brian Moore piped up, 'There are an awful lot of isobars about – and I've been in every one of them.'

## VIP

Not all rugby tours are pleasurable. Dissatisfaction with facilities is an occupational hazard for rugby tourists. The story is told that, on the Lions tour to New Zealand in 1993, the secretary of the touring party, Bob Weighill, asked for an extra pat of butter to accompany his bread roll. He took umbrage when he was told this would not be possible. 'Do you know who I am?'

'No, sir.'

The waiter listened impassively as Mr Weighill listed his auspicious catalogue of titles. Then he softly replied, 'And do you know who I am?'

'No.'

'I'm in charge of the butter.'

## I only have eyes for you

In 1992, Scotland toured Australia. Flanker Carl Hogg was making his debut for Scotland in the Test match. It was a dream come true for Hogg and he was really keyed up to play against the world champions. The Australians do things in style and they had XXXX dancing girls warming up the crowd. During the anthems Hogg was standing beside Doddie Weir. When 'Flower of Scotland' was played, Hogg had tears in his eyes. Weir said to him, 'Look at them, little do they know what they're in for later.'

Hogg replied: 'I'm with you, Dod.'

'Oh, Hoggy, they're not going to know what hit them!'

'Yup, we're going to f**king smash them right up.'

Doddie turned to the debutant in bewilderment: 'What are you talking about?'

'Those Aussies, come the first whistle, we're going to flatten them, destroy them.'

'Are you mad?' asked Doddie. 'I wasn't talking about getting stuck into the Aussies, open your eyes, I'm talking about the girls in front of us.'

## Agony uncle
On tour to England, David Campese took a taxi back to the team hotel with a few of the other players after a drinking session one evening. The taxi driver was a bit obese and was also 'hygenically challenged', with a less than enticing aroma emanating from his body. In addition, he recounted a tale of woe about his lack of success with the opposite sex. After the Aussie lads paid their fare, the taxi driver said, 'How about a tip?' Before anyone could even thinking of reaching into their pockets for a second time, Campo interjected, 'Certainly. Start using a deodorant and you might have some chance with the Sheilas.'

## Lassie come home
In the 1990s, the great Australian team were on tour. They got into the airport and the whole squad had disembarked and were waiting in the baggage hall by the carousel. Bags were going around and around, and the players were waiting patiently when they noticed a drugs squad officer with a sniffer dog in tow. He let the dog off the lead and it ran to the carousel and bounded onto the bags, rummaging around. Jason Little was awestruck: 'Isn't that wonderful?'

'Why, Jason?'

'Well, isn't it great? The dog's looking for the blind man's luggage.'

# Wish You Were Here

## It's not the winning that counts

On the 1989 Lions tour to Australia, the players were invited on a rare day off to the Royal Perth Yacht Club. It was just after Australia had lost the America's Cup to the US. Not all the tour party were present, but among the group were three Welsh backs. The president of the yacht club was showing them around the club and took them onto the *Kookaburra 2*, the boat that the hopes of the nation had rested on in the race, only to be thwarted when the American boat *Stars and Stripes* won the head-to-head race. The captain of *Kookaburra 2* was then introduced to the players. One of the Welsh threesome innocently asked, 'Do a bit of racing then, do you?'

'Yeah, mate. In fact, we've just been in the America's Cup where we sailed against the Americans.'

The second Welsh back: 'How did you get on, then?'

'We came second.'

The third Welshman interjected, 'Second. That's bloody good, isn't it?!'

## The old man and the seat

The All Blacks toured Wales in 1989. They were intrigued by the Welsh fans. Most of the time the Kiwis were based in the Grand Hotel in Cardiff, as most of the club sides were accessible from there. One day early on in the tour, they were walking down the high street getting a breath of fresh air and there was an elderly man sitting on a bench. He recognised the rugby aristocrats immediately and asked, 'Oh, boys, who have you got tomorrow?'

'Cardiff,' they replied.

'Cardiff will beat you,' he said. 'Cardiff are a good side. They will beat you.'

Cardiff lost.

A few days later, the players met the old man again. 'Who are you playing next?'

'Newport.'

'Newport, good side, tough side, Rodney Parade, wide ground, they will beat you.'

Newport lost. The following morning they met the old man and he asked his by now customary question. They replied, 'Neath.'

'Neath are the Welsh champions this year. They will beat you.'

He was wrong again, but the players were too polite to mention this when the familiar ritual was repeated the next time they met him and he confidently predicted, 'Llanelli, at home at Stradey, big crowd. They will beat you.'

Again, the All Blacks won. Finally it came to the match they had all been really looking forward to – the Test match against Wales. They again met the old man.

'Who have you got tomorrow?'

'Wales.'

'Oh, Wales, they're bloody crap, you'll beat them!'

## Should old acquaintance be forgot

That same year, the Lions toured Australia. During a night on the town, David Sole was at the bar when he spotted someone he recognised from back home in Scotland. He rushed up and greeted his 'friend' effusively: 'What brings you over to Oz?'

'I live here,' was the reply, in a tone that, had David been less inebriated, would have told him that the man had absolutely no idea who the rugby player was and in an accent that would have told him that he had not an ounce of Scottish blood in him.

'Didn't you used to have a beard at one time?' asked Sole.

'No.'

'You used to be taller. You must have shrunk but it's great to see you all the same, Sam.'

'My name isn't Sam, it's Cliff.'

'Good God! You've changed your name as well.'

## Donal's gems

Put-downs were a particular speciality of Donal Lenihan. During the 1989 Lions tour of Australia, Lenihan's ready wit was to the fore on a number of occasions. At one stage Bridgend's Mike Griffiths ventured, 'Can I ask a stupid question?'

'Better than anyone I know,' answered Lenihan.

Another time the touring party were driving through Sydney when they passed a couple coming out of a church after being married. In all earnestness, Jeremy Guscott asked, 'Why do people throw rice at weddings?'

Lenihan replied immediately, 'Because rocks hurt.' He then turned defence into attack: 'Why do you think they're getting married, Jeremy?'

'I suppose, Donal, it's because they love each other.'

'I wanted a reason and you gave me an excuse.'

Jeremy replied, 'Don't be so cynical. Marriage is a great institution.'

Donal nodded his head in agreement: 'Marriage is a great institution all right. It's holy deadlock.'

Scott Hastings grew impatient when his brother Gavin seemed to prefer playing tennis or going windsurfing with Ieuan Evans rather than with him. Lenihan commented, 'Ieuan's like the brother Gavin never had.'

'What about me?' asked Scott.

'You're the brother he did have,' responded Lenihan.

The capacity for put-downs seems to be a common trait in the Lenihan family. After Ireland lost to Australia in the World Cup in 1987, Donal rang home. As a result of the time difference, the match was shown live on Irish television at 6 a.m. His mother had seen the match and knew the result already. Instead of offering him sympathy, she said, 'Anyone stupid enough to play rugby at six o'clock in the morning deserves to lose.'

After defeating Australian Capital Territories 27–11 in 1989,

Lenihan brought the touring Lions party to the Friends of Ireland bar, where they were greeted by a priest. After much liquid refreshment, it was time for the team to return to their hotel. The priest bade them farewell. Slightly under the influence, one of the 'star players', Andy Robinson, told the minister he was wearing his collar back to front.

'I'm a father, Andrew,' said the priest.

'I've got kids myself,' replied Robinson.

'No, I'm the father to hundreds of people in this area,' explained the priest.

'Really? In that case it's not your collar you should be wearing back to front, it's your bloody trousers!'

Rob Andrew was the only one to put one over on Lenihan on the tour. On a night off he invited Donal to *La Traviata*. Thinking they were going to a nice Italian restaurant, Lenihan agreed. What he failed to realise was that they'd been given complimentary tickets to the opera!

### Whatever the weather

Gavin Hastings recalls watching the news on the television during the 1987 World Cup in New Zealand; the newscaster was reading out the temperatures for towns throughout New Zealand:

Auckland 20 Wellington 18

Christchurch 14 Invercargill 10

Palmerstown North 16 Wangaum 12

One of the Scottish props walked in, saw the TV and said, 'Crikey, these scores are pretty close!'

### A holy show

In the 1987 World Cup, the Irish team were coached by the late Mick Doyle. Doyler decided he was going to get into shape on the trip because he was two stone overweight. He started to train with the backs and when the lads saw this they stepped up a gear. At the end of the session, Doyler was in bits. Later that night Donal Lenihan heard that he had been taken to hospital. As captain, Donal went to see him that evening in hospital in a taxi. He was in the front seat and Syd Millar and Mick Molloy were in the back. At one stage in the conversation, Syd said Mick's wife Lynne had been on the phone and was very concerned about him and wanted to come down under to see him. Then he said his girlfriend Mandy was very worried about him and she too wanted to travel to see him. The Maori taxi driver turned to Donal and said with real feeling, 'That stuff about holy Catholic Ireland is a load of crap!'

When Donal got back from the hospital, Brian Spillane asked, 'Did he have a girl or a boy?'

Some years later, at a dinner, Donal told this story to a charming woman with an English accent whom he had never met before, nor had he any idea who she was, except that she was very well versed in rugby matters. It turned out to be Doyler's ex-wife Lynne!

## Sheepish

On the 1983 Lions tour to New Zealand, at breakfast in Wanganui during the first week, Colin Deans rushed into the dining room and said, 'Quick, quick, I'm late for training. Can you please get me some toast and rashers of bacon?'

The waitress apologised and said, 'You won't believe it – we're out of bacon.'

Deans looked aghast and stared at her in disbelief: 'Three million sheep in New Zealand – how can you be out of bacon?'

## Show courts

It is important to have light moments on a tour, whether it is with club, country or the Lions. One effort to break the monotony during a rugby tour is 'a court session', where players are judged by their peers and given an appropriate punishment for their transgressions. These are good innocent fun and part of the ethos of tours, because they certainly contribute towards improved morale. They generally involve taking in more than a modicum of drink.

People are fined for different reasons and the more fines they get, the more drink they enjoy. Players are charged for incidents in training or in matches, for example somebody who dropped the ball a few times in training might be charged with being a 'butterfingers'. The fine might be to drink a bottle of beer without using their hands. On the 1993 Lions tour, Judge Paul Rendall sentenced Scott Hastings to listen to two hours of Richard Clayderman tapes on his personal stereo after he was found guilty of having his hair cut in a style that was 'an affront to what little hair Graham Dawe had left'.

At one stage on that tour, Nick Popplewell was the judge, Stuart Barnes was the defending barrister and Brian Moore was the prosecutor. Things got unexpectedly serious one night before the First Test when Moore suddenly started talking about tactics. He said, 'I've got an idea to improve our chances on this tour.'

Stuart Barnes immediately said, 'Great. When are you leaving?'

## Ebony and ivory

Towards the end of January 1981, 44 Irish rugby players were written to by the IRFU requesting that they indicate if they would be available for the Irish short tour of South Africa in May and June. The letters went out amidst a welter of controversy as political, clerical and media people objected to the notion of Ireland having sporting contact with South Africa. A number of players declined the invitation. Perhaps the bravest decision not to travel of all was that of Hugo MacNeill, who was just establishing his international place at the time. It took remarkable moral courage for an emerging star to turn down his first overseas tour with his country. Hugo did manage to extract some fun from the touring situation. Around about this time there was a lot of money being offered under the table for players to play in exhibition games in South Africa. One of the ways Hugo sometimes wound up his colleagues in the Irish team was to ring them up, put on a South African accent and offer them £25,000 to play in such a match. It was always interesting to see who showed great interest, but he's not going to name names!

A depleted Irish side toured South Africa. The tour saw one of the great wind-ups of Irish rugby. One Saturday, Freddie McLennan was 'duty boy' (the player in charge of informing teammates about travel arrangements etc. for a particular day during a tour abroad; each player took it in turn). The squad had been given the day off and had to decide how to spend it. Freddie, himself a keen golfer, offered two choices. They could either go for a game of golf or take a trip around Johannesburg harbour. Eighteen players favoured the harbour trip on the basis that they could play golf any time but would not always get the chance to do some sightseeing in Johannesburg. The next morning the players were ready at 8 a.m. for their trip around the harbour, only to be told that since the city was 5,000 feet above sea level it didn't have a harbour and the nearest seaside was a massive bus trip away.

## A Passage to Romania

In 1980, the year Jimmy Carter had arranged a boycott of the Moscow Olympics because of Russia's invasion of Afghanistan, Leinster, under Mick Doyle and Mick 'the Cud' Cuddy, toured Romania. The Cud is a master of the art of the malapropism. One of his many classic comments is, 'There were so many people they were coming out of the woodroom.'

One of the players on the tour was Jim Glennon, who was elected to the Irish parliament in 2002. As a player, Jim always gave 150 per cent. Although he is not an arrogant person, he does make one proud boast: 'Nobody used his arse better in the lineout than Jim Glennon did!' Glennon was never a great lineout winner, but was very hard to get lineout ball from. He formed a very effective second-row partnership with George Wallace for Leinster. They were christened 'Urbi et Orbi' by Mick Doyle.

A vivid memory for Glennon is of going to see Romania play Russia with Phil Orr and George Wallace. The Russians were staying in the same hotel as Leinster but on a different floor. That night the three amigos met up with the Russian captain and invited him and his colleagues up to their room for a jar. They had stared disaster in the face earlier when they discovered that there was only one bottle of whiskey in the hotel. Worse still, that bottle was in the Cud's room and not intended for public consumption. The Cud was annoyed to put it mildly when he discovered it 'missing'.

The next morning the manager of the Russian team came into the lobby and asked to speak to 'the leader of the Irish delegation' and invited Leinster to tour in Russia. It was a pretty strange spectacle because the Russians had KGB types following them everywhere, watching their every move. Glennon thought this invitation might provide the key to a rapprochement with the Cud, so he headed in before the Russian delegation to explain the situation. The Cud was not impressed. He said, 'Look, Glennon, would you ever bleep off and tell them Russians to bleep off and while you're at it tell them to bleep off out of Afghanistan as well!'

Leinster were confident of better treatment when they made a tour to Venice. It was a pretty bizarre event. They travelled to the match by boat. They kept to one side and their opponents to the other. The boat brought both teams back together and the meal didn't start until a quarter past midnight. The mayor of Venice invited the officials and a few of the players to a reception in Venice's most prestigious building. The Leinster delegation were all dressed up in their official blazers. As they went into this very impressive building, they noticed there was a sheet covering a table. They were all a bit taken aback when the mayor, who was a Communist, strolled out in the most casual of clothes, a grandad shirt and jeans. Then the sheet was taken off the table and they saw that their reception was in fact a few bottles of soft drinks. The officials were less than impressed but the players thought it was absolutely hilarious.

Glennon was involved in Mick Doyle's first and last representative games as coach – in 1979 when Leinster played Cheshire and in 1987 when Ireland played Australia respectively. He lays claim to an unusual distinction: he once saw Doyle speechless. After his heart attack during the '87 World Cup, Doyler rejoined the Irish team after a ten-day stay in hospital. They were staying in a motel-type place. A few of the lads, known on the tour as the 'amigos', had been out late one night and were sneaking furtively in. There was an uncarpeted staircase outside Doyler's room and he was woken up by the activity. He recognised one of the voices. The next day the culprit was given a right ticking off in front of the whole squad. As Doyler delivered his attack, the player in question stood and listened, but when the coach had finished the bad boy said, 'Jaysus, Doyler, there's none so pure as a converted hoor.' Doyler was left too stunned to speak.

Old rugby players never die – they simply have their balls taken away. Even after his retirement Glennon, to his own surprise, continued to grace the world's playing fields. When he finished playing in 1988, he got the most unexpected invitations to tour. The golden oldies idea was really taking off. He got a phone call from Moss Keane in June of that year enquiring if he was free for the last weekend in August. When Jim said he was, Moss told him to keep it free. Jim forgot all about it until the last Wednesday in August, when he got another call from Moss. Moss told him that he had been invited to play in an exhibition match across the water for a Lions golden oldies side against a junior team and although he had been given the plane ticket he was unable to travel. He was going to ring the organiser and tell him he couldn't make it but that he would be meeting Jim later that day and would attempt to persuade him to travel. Shortly afterwards, Glennon got a phone call from a panic-stricken secretary apologising profusely for the short notice but wondering would he be willing to play instead of Moss. Jim 'reluctantly' agreed. On the plane over, he was joined by Phil Orr, Willie Duggan and Fergus Slattery. It was a fabulous weekend. Glennon was the only 'non-Lion' on the team. His partner in the second row was Allan Martin of Wales. After the match, the pair were chatting in the bath when Martin asked him out of the blue, 'What about Stockholm?' He went on to explain that there was a golden oldies match there the following weekend, Thursday to Monday, but he couldn't travel; would Jim be interested? When Glennon said yes, Allan told Jim just to leave it with him. On the Monday, Jim rang Moss to thank him for the wonderful weekend and asked him why he had left it so late to tell them he couldn't make it. Moss answered, 'Because I didn't want some hoor from England to take my place.'

Two days later, Jim got a phone call from a different panic-stricken secretary apologising profusely for the short notice but wondering would he be willing to play instead of Allan. This time Jim made him sweat a bit more and told him he wasn't sure if he would be able to make it because he had other commitments, but he rang him back less than an hour later and agreed to the trip. On the plane over, he was again joined by Orr, Duggan and Slattery. Also on the trip were J.P.R. Williams and Jim Renwick, among others. It was an absolutely fabulous weekend. On the Tuesday morning, Jim rang to thank Alan for putting it his way. When he asked him why he had left it so late to tell them he couldn't make it, he replied, 'Because I didn't want some hoor from England to take my place.'

## John O'Desperate

John 'O'Desperate' O'Driscoll is the consummate gentleman but he liked to enjoy himself on tour. He was a very committed, driven player but a real Jekyll and Hyde character. His party piece was to hang out of windows late at night. During Ireland's tour of South Africa in 1981, this got a bit boring after a number of weeks. For the sake of variety, he decided he would hang someone else out of the window, so one night he dangled Terry Kennedy by the legs outside the hotel window – 17 storeys up. It's the only time his teammates ever saw Terry quiet. Then Willie Duggan came into the room, puffing his cigarette, with a bottle of beer in his hand and with his matted hair that hadn't been combed since the tour started. As Willie was such a senior player and a close friend of John's, people assumed he would talk some sense into him. All he said to John before turning and walking out was: 'O'Driscoll, you don't have the guts to let him go.' He was right, too!

## The Cotton diet

The English prop Fran Cotton's nickname was 'Noddy' because he liked his sleep. He had a serious health scare on the Lions tour to South Africa in 1980. He was erroneously diagnosed as having suffered a heart attack during the match against the Proteas. It transpired he had suffered an attack of pericarditis – inflammation of tissue around the heart. When Fran's English hooker Peter Wheeler, 'Wheelbrace', heard that the world's most famous heart transplant surgeon Christiaan Barnard had, jokingly, offered to perform his services on Fran, he said, 'They would never have found a heart big enough.'

When he was told by his doctors that he was out of shape because of too much red meat, fine wine and white bread, Fran replied, 'Fine. I'll give up white bread then.' When he returned to England, he went for a check-up. His concerned doctor told him to give up smoking, drinking, eating rich food and chasing women. 'Will that help me to live longer?' asked Fran.

'Hopefully,' said the doctor, 'but I'm not sure. You see, no one has tried it yet.'

His Lions teammates sent him a get-well card. It read, 'Gone but not for Cotton.'

A few months later, Cotton went back to his doctor. The doctor said: 'This is the diet you must follow. Three lettuce leaves, a slice of dry toast and a glass of orange juice twice a day.'

Fran replied: 'I see. Now is that before meals or after?'

## Bum deal

Fran's captain on the tour to South Africa was Bill Beaumont. Uniquely among the forwards on the tour, every time he went into a ruck, the ball came back on the Lions' side. Bill was not the most mobile forward but he still managed to get around; not the greatest lineout jumper yet he still managed to win the ball. He was not an awesome forward in the Wade Dooley sense, though he had a tremendous ability to use his own physique. He was always a great scrummager. He was nicknamed 'Sun Bum' on that tour because he had plenty of padding in those places which made him ideal for scrummaging. He was given the name by Peter Wheeler. Sunday was always their day off training and Wheelbrace arranged T-shirts for the squad which read: 'Sun Bum's Sunday Sessions Side'. Beaumont's backside was also jokingly known on the tour as 'the outboard motor'.

## Welsh wisdom

The 1980 Lions tour took place in the era when you paid for your own telephone calls home. The Welsh players had three great tricks devised so they never had to pay for a telephone. Plan A was to charm the hotel receptionist into giving them the secret code they could use to make calls without having them charged to them. Plan B was to distract the receptionist and for one of them to sneak in behind the desk and steal all their telephone bills. Plan C was, when a journalist asked for an interview, to trade it for a phone call.

Best of all, though, for getting freebies was when they went to the Adidas factory. Each player was allowed to pick a bag of their choice and stuff it with gear. Most players selected the most stylish bags and filled them up. All the Welsh guys without exception took the biggest bags in the shop and walked out with half the gear in the factory! In 1983, when the Scottish players were chosen to tour with the Lions to New Zealand, the advice 1980 tourist John Beattie gave them was: 'Be sure and stay close to the Welsh when they visit the Adidas factory!'

One night the Welsh contingent did a classic wind-up on the English winger Mike Slemen, who was the leading try-scorer on the tour. All of them gathered in the one room and one of them rang him up pretending to be from the BBC World Service, with a suitable posh accent. The Welshmen fed him a lot of compliments and he started blowing his own trumpet, claiming that he was probably one of the best players on the tour. Eventually the Welsh lads could take no more and shouted, 'Slemen, you're a useless f\*\*ker!' The Englishman was mortified that he had been caught out so badly.

## Panic stations

The 1980 Lions were preparing for what was effectively a fifth Test against one of South Africa's top provincial sides, Northern Transvaal. One of their centres that day was Ray Gravell from Wales. He always got very nervous before big matches and tried to cope by singing nationalistic Welsh songs, crying and getting sick, although not necessarily in that order! Before this particular match, his gumshield went missing. He basically gave an ultimatum to the team that he was not going to play unless it was found. The result was that, instead of the normal serious preparation for the match, every member of the touring party was emptying bags and looking under benches for Ray's gumshield while he cried, sang and got sick. Fortunately they did eventually find it – in Ray's own gear bag!

### Flipper and the Commanchero

In the history of Irish rugby there has never been a bigger shock than coach Noel Murphy's decision in 1979 to drop the European Player of the Year, Tony Ward, for the First Test against Australia and replace him with the virtually unknown Ollie Campbell. Campbell grabbed the opportunity with both hands: he produced a dazzling display and went on to establish himself as one of the top names in world rugby.

Exactly a year later, fate decreed that the three protagonists were to be brought together again. Murphy was coaching the Lions on their tour to South Africa, where his non-Irish players had to get used to his rather unusual instructions, such as 'Spread out in a bunch!' Campbell was the Lions' chief place-kicker as well as out-half. When he sustained an injury, it was Murphy who would tell Ward that he was in because Campbell was out. One of South Africa's main newspapers, the *Rand Daily Mail*, made Ward's dramatic summons to the touring party front-page news, totally relegating a major political story of the day, a government decision to establish an industrial zone in Northern Transvaal, to a poor second place – a tribute to Ward's reputation but also evidence, if any were needed, of the extraordinary importance of rugby in South African society.

With the Ward–Campbell debate still raging, Campbell would have been happier if Ward had been back home in Ireland. Not only did Ward play in the First Test, he scored 18 points, which was then a Lions individual points-scoring record in a Test match. Was Campbell to have no escape from this guy?

Ward was a sub to Campbell in the Third Test in Port Elizabeth. To his horror, he discovered in the dressing-room that he had forgotten his boots. It was too late to retrieve them from the team hotel. His problem was exacerbated by the fact that nobody had a spare pair of boots to lend him. He consoled himself with the thought that he probably would not need them.

## Wish You Were Here

The seating arrangements for the subs that day were bizarre, to say the least. They were to sit in the very top row of the stadium. As the match began, Ward was making the long journey up countless flights of stairs with John Robbie when he heard somebody shouting for him. Campbell jokes about a lost opportunity to scuttle his rival's career. He was injured in the very first moments of the match and was pumping blood. He still has a small scar on his face as a souvenir. It was panic stations all round. John Robbie got a pair of boots from a ball boy for Wardie to wear. At size nine they were too big for him but an even more serious problem was that the studs were moulded. The pitch was waterlogged that day, and even if they had been the right size, they would have been a disaster in the conditions, but they were all he had at the time. Campbell played the rest of the match in the end, but he jokes that if only he had known, he'd have been straight off and Ward wouldn't have got his boots! It would have been Wardie's ultimate nightmare and his reputation would have been destroyed at a stroke!

Ward immediately struck up a close friendship with Scotland's Jim Renwick. On the tour, Ward nearly lost his life. He had been relaxing with the squad at the Umhlanga Rocks Indian Ocean resort north of Durban and went for a swim. He is a poor swimmer and the undertow was very strong; it carried him out and he was literally out of his depth. He started shouting and his fellow Irish international John O'Driscoll, who is a very strong swimmer, and the lifeguard rescued him. Having just had the scariest experience of his life, Ward might have expected sympathy, but Renwick's immediate response was to christen him 'Flipper'.

Jim's nickname was 'the Commanchero', after the song of the same name. The following season Ireland were to play Scotland at Murrayfield. Ward arranged to have a telegram sent to Renwick in the team hotel on the day before the match which read: 'Commanchero beware. Flipper's in town.' About an hour before the game, the teams went out to inspect the pitch. Part of the psychological warfare that goes on before a major international is that a player seldom makes eye contact with the opposition. They keep their heads down and count the daisies rather than look an opposing player in the face. The Irish were coming out of the tunnel with the Scottish players, but neither Renwick nor Ward could stop themselves from looking at each other out of the corner of their eye. Ward smiled, feeling he had one up on him because of the telegram. When they went back inside after the pitch inspection, the secretary of the Scottish Rugby Football Union came into the Irish dressing-room, saying: 'Telegram for Mr Ward.' It read simply: 'Flipper shut your zipper. The Commanchero.'

### Don't cry for me Argentina

Willie Anderson will probably always be remembered as the player who precipitated an international diplomatic incident. He was on a tour of Argentina with the Penguins in 1980 when he took a shine to the Argentinian flag and decided to claim it as his own. The only problem was that he was caught and spent a few harrowing months in prison.

Willie met Denis Thatcher some years later and told him that he could have told Maggie Thatcher that the Argentinians were scrapping for a war. There was an amusing postscript to the incident many years later. Willie was attending the Bermuda Classic and the Argentinians were playing the Americans. The ball went out of play and came in his direction. As he went to retrieve it, he heard one of the Argentinians say, 'Give us back the ball there, Willie, and while you're at it give us back our flag as well!'

### Can do

On Ireland's tour to Australia in 1979, the Tuesday before the First Test, Ireland were playing Queensland in what was effectively a Test match for the tourists. Ireland won. After the match, there were a lot of barbecues. The Irish players were watching them from out of their window and started singing 'Waltzing Matilda'. The Aussies began throwing beer cans at them but the boys in green had the last laugh because many of the cans were half-full, so they grabbed the cans, drank the beer and threw the cans back at them!

The Australian press rubbished Ireland's chances of winning the First Test. One headline read: 'Ireland To Be Paddywhacked Into Rugby Oblivion'. Ireland won 27–12! The rugby correspondent of the paper in question ate humble pie. The only comparable story he could think of to explain his misjudgement came at the turn of the century. Two men, Mr Marks and Mr Smith, were talking. Mr Marks outlined his plans for a new shop and asked Mr Smith to be his partner. Mr Smith replied, 'Nah. It'll never work.' Mr Marks found a new partner – Mr Spencer. He concluded by saying the result was history – just like the Test match!

## The black market

Top Irish club St Mary's toured Russia in 1977. It was a strange environment at the time; they had two Russian police going everywhere with them, keeping tabs on everything they did. It was the pre-glasnost, pre-perestroika era and everybody in Russia was mad for Western goods, especially jeans. They had all their team blazers and jumpers and O'Neills (a native Irish clothing company) playing gear, so they were able to sell off their jeans for about £100 in today's money. But their masterstroke was to convince the Russians that O'Neills was Irish for Adidas! That tour cost the players virtually nothing as a result of their black market activities.

## The odd couple

In any roll of honour of the characters in world rugby, at the top of the list are Moss Keane and Willie Duggan. Moss Keane folklore grows every day. Since his capture on 8 February 1983,

Shergar has been at stud in the Middle East, galloping around the Scottish Highlands, peacefully grazing in a Channel Islands meadow, part of the Mafia, involved in a Kentucky killing and even giving riding lessons to runaway British aristocrat Lord Lucan. Likewise, if even a fraction of the stories about Moss were true, he would have needed a brewery of his own to supply him with Guinness, broken down more doors than most people have eaten hot dinners and generally been responsible for extraordinary levels of mirth and mayhem.

Moss toured with the Lions in New Zealand in 1977. After their Second Test victory, the Lions threw the party to beat all parties in the team hotel. It was soon discovered that one of their players was missing. According to legend, when everyone else expressed concern about him, Moss said he knew where the missing person was – next door with his girlfriend. Moss was dispatched to bring the guilty party back – though given strict instructions not to break down any doors. (His nickname on that tour was 'Rent-a-Storm' so the decree seemed more than justified.) The rest of the squad listened to a slight flurry next door and moments later Moss came in the door with the missing player under his arm, completely naked and squirming like a fish on a hook. Under the other arm he held the player's girlfriend in a similar state of undress and embarrassment. Moss, in his best Kerry accent, boomed out, 'To be sure, did you be wanting the two of them?'

In fairness, Moss did try to keep the players intellectually stimulated on the tour. As he finished his last drink, Moss called for silence in the bar and asked a question: who played soccer for Scotland and cricket for England? Everyone was left scratching their heads and no one could figure out the answer. Finally, just before he walked out the door, Moss answered his own question: 'Denis Law and Ian Botham!'

Wish You Were Here

## Dug-in
Willie Duggan was a star of the Lions tour in 1977. However, he did not have a great interest in the theoretical side of the game. He fell asleep during a team talk in Sydney on Ireland's 1979 tour to Australia. Coach Noel Murphy sarcastically apologised to him afterwards: 'I'm sorry for boring you, Willie.'

## More sex, please, we're British
Media reports often blow events on tour out of proportion. In 1977, during the Lions tour to New Zealand, the British media were full of stories about the Lions team having wild sex parties involving dozens of local women picked up around the town. This was a time when 'safe sex' meant a padded headboard on the bed. Bobby Windsor was furious. When he read reports of the game and its aftermath, he demanded to know where the orgies were talking place and why he hadn't been invited!

Bobby was less than impressed by some of the food on offer at an official reception. He made his feelings known to the chef: 'It's not often you get the soup and the wine at the same temperature.'

When the Lions stopped off at a roadside café during a long coach drive, Windsor complained to Phil Bennett, 'I went into the kitchen here and, do you know, there isn't a single bluebottle in there. They're all married with kids.' Windsor was even more irate when he tasted the food. He asked the chef, 'What do you do about salmonella?' The chef replied, 'I fry it in a little batter.'

In the team hotel one morning, Bobby was not satisfied with some of the food. At one stage he called over the waiter and said, 'These eggs are awful.'

The waiter casually replied, 'Don't blame me. I only laid the table.' Later that day Windsor had another encounter with the same waiter. Bobby was early at the table for dinner but when

241

the waiter came to take his order he told him he wasn't ready to order until his friends arrived. The waiter sarcastically replied, 'Oh, you must be the table for two, sir.'

## Let us pray

It wouldn't be accurate to say the Irish team were an ecumenical bunch but there were times religion brought them together. Ireland became the first team from the northern hemisphere to beat Australia on home soil in 1967. After winning on the Saturday, the boys in green had a great celebration, and all went to Mass on the Sunday evening. Although it was the evening after the night before, one of the lads feel asleep. During the most solemn point of the Mass, he suddenly shouted out from his slumber, 'Hallelujah.'

On the tour to New Zealand in 1976, the team doctor, Bob O'Connell, organised Mass for the Irish team at Palmerston North on a holy day of obligation for Catholics. As they could not get Mass elsewhere, it was decided to invite a priest in to them, and that everybody would go to Mass. The Catholics knew to bring change for the collection, but the others didn't, with the result that the priest got a 'silent collection' from the Protestants. He was thrilled and wrote to all the Irish papers telling them what a wonderful bunch the Irish squad were and such fabulous ambassadors for their country.

They had great characters in the squad, none more so than Brendan Foley. He is the father of current Irish star Anthony 'Axel' Foley. At one stage on that tour, he came down to the foyer of the hotel which had a big fountain. He went into the middle of it to do some fishing. He didn't catch anything! After that he was known as 'Foley never caught a fish'.

Phil O'Callaghan had been recalled for the tour. He looked a bit older than the rest of the Irish squad. A Kiwi journalist asked him who he was. Philo answered: 'I'm Ireland's secret weapon.'

On the last game of the tour, Ireland played Fiji. The pitch had 18 inches of mud. Frogs were jumping on the playing surface during the match. Tony Ensor ran over for a try but there was so much mud he ran over the dead-ball line and Ireland lost the try. Ireland defeated their hosts 8–0. Normally there are shouts of joy after an Irish team selection is announced. The Fiji game was no exception. However, so humid was the climate that this time all the hurrahs came from the players not selected. Moss Keane was one of them. It was much more interesting looking out on the most beautiful ocean in the world than watching the match. As the squad departed, they heard Moss shouting at them and thought he was just wishing them well. Then they discovered he was drowning!

Ireland's experiences were not unique. When England played Fiji in the early 1990s, the English players were very intimidated by the crowd and the sea of black faces. Will Carling is said to have remarked, 'Jesus Christ – we'll be lucky to get out of here alive.'

Jeremy Guscott immediately stepped in and said, 'Speak for yourself.'

## The Lion King

The most successful British Lions team of all time was that which toured South Africa in 1974. Their overall record in their 22 matches read: won 21, drawn 1, lost 0, points for 729, points against 207. After their 12–3 victory in the First Test, skipper Willie John McBride warned his fellow forwards to expect a bruising encounter: 'You have not seen anything yet. They will throw everything at you, even the kitchen sink.'

One night on the '74 Lions tour, a group of players were partying and disturbed other guests in their hotel in the middle of the night. An undiplomatic war broke out. The tiny hotel manager tried to keep the peace. Two scantily clad players were parading around the corridors and he roared at them to get back into their rooms. Not liking his attitude, they told him with all due lack of politeness what to do with himself. The

That sink-ing feeling

manager's threat to ring the police met with no reaction. At this point, along came Willie John McBride. The manager thought his problems were solved at the sight of the Lions captain arriving. When McBride seemed to be ignoring the matter, the manager repeated his threat to call the police. Willie John called him forward with a tilt of his head. The manager breathed a sigh of relief. His threat had worked. He was in for a big disappointment, as McBride bent down to him and whispered, 'How many will there be?'

Willie John went back to the party. Some time later a group of riot police arrived with their dogs. Again Willie John intervened decisively. He went down to the coffee machine, bought some milk and gave it to the dogs, and then invited the police to join the party. They did, and had the night of their lives.

When the Lions won the series in 1974, a magnificent party was staged at the hotel. The festive spirit got a little out of hand

and every fire extinguisher and water hose in the hotel was set off. The problem was that nobody thought to turn them off, the result being that the next morning the hotel could have done with the services of Noah's ark. The tour manager was summoned the next morning by the hotel manager to explain the actions of his team. He had gone to bed early and had no idea what had happened until he discovered himself thigh-deep in water. They half-walked, half-swam up to Willie John's room and prepared to knock on the door only to discover that the door had been a casualty of the flood. To their astonishment, McBride was calmly sitting on his bed as it bobbed around on the water, puffing contentedly on his pipe. The hotel manager lost control and launched into a vicious tirade. Finally, Willie John replied, 'Can I ask you one question?'

'What?'

'Is there anybody dead?'

## Joyriders

Another famous player on the '74 Lions tour was Fergus Slattery. An auctioneer by profession, Slats was not sold many dummies on the field. A product of Blackrock College, he was capped over 60 times for Ireland as an open-side wing forward (a then world record for a flanker) between 1970 and 1984, scoring 3 international tries. The classic story told about Slattery goes back to an African trip. After a British Lions tour fixture in Rhodesia, a celebratory dinner was organised. The then Rhodesian prime minister Ian Smith arrived to make a speech. Shortly after, two Irish players, Dick Milliken and Slats, decided to return to their hotel. Having consumed beverages stronger than orange juice, they were feeling particularly adventurous. As they walked out, they noticed just outside the entrance to the club was a beautiful Cadillac with black-tinted windows. They decided to borrow the car and go for a drive. After they had been driving around for a few minutes, the partition behind the front seats slid across and the Prime Minister asked, 'Are you gentlemen looking for a job?'

In June 1983, Slats went to Barcelona to play an exhibition game against a French selection with the Wolfhounds. The match was to be played at midday. The evening before the game, Fergus was looking for somebody to go out with him for a night on the town. Under the circumstances, nobody wanted to take up his invitation, knowing the tough conditions awaiting them the next day, but eventually he recruited the replacement prop forward. The next morning the two lads returned from their adventures as the French team were heading out to train! Fergus was not a bit fazed. On the bus to the game Phil Orr was taken ill and, to his horror, the partying sub had to take his place. Slats played like a man inspired, but nobody had ever seen anyone suffer on the pitch like his partner!

## Bachelor boy

Irish scrum-half Johnny Moloney also toured with the Lions in South Africa in 1974. Near the end of the tour, he was summoned before the players' informal court. Johnny was charged with a very serious offence – he hadn't 'enjoyed conjugal relations' with any woman on the tour, even though he was still single at the time. In his defence, Johnny said, very unconvincingly, that he had in fact slept with two women. Tom Grace said immediately, 'Shagger.'

Shortly after they returned, Mick Quinn saw Johnny at a reception with his girlfriend at the time, subsequently his wife, Miriam, and he shouted over at him, 'How's it going, Shagger?' Miriam discreetly asked Quinn later why he had called him Shagger. Quinn told her that what goes on on a tour is sacred and there was no way he could disclose any intimate details about Johnny's behaviour. Moloney had some explaining to do that night.

## Verbal Lynch mob

One of the great characters of rugby is the Ireland and Lions prop Sean Lynch. Lynchie was on the Irish tour to Argentina in 1970. All the players were attending a dinner. A Lord Somebody was to be the main dignitary. Before he arrived, the players were told that he had Parkinson's disease and to be patient as it would take him a long time to walk to the dinner table. After what seemed like half an hour, the Lord eventually made it to his seat. He was sitting beside Lynchie and said, 'Well, Mr Lynch, are you enjoying your tour?'

Lynchie replied, 'Yes, Mr Parkinson, I am.'

Lynch was one of the surprise stars of the Lions tour in 1971. He was to play a more central role than anybody could have foreseen at the start of the tour. The week before the First Test in Dunedin, the Lions had lost their two first-choice props, Ray McLoughlin and Sandy Carmichael, with long-term injuries in the infamous 'battle of Christchurch'. The match confirmed an old adage: 'New Zealand rugby is a colourful game – you get all black and blue.'

Lynchie's prop partner was the squat Scot, Ian McLauchlan, 'Mighty Mouse'. One of his opponents scornfully dismissed him with the words, 'You'll be Mickey Mouse by the time I've finished with you.' Yet it was the Lions who had the last laugh, winning 9–3. The crowd's silence after the game bore eloquent testimony to the scale of the shock.

The series hinged on the Fourth Test. For both the Lions and the All Blacks, it was do or die. The All Blacks had been victorious in the Second Test and the Lions had won the Third Test 13–3 in Wellington, thanks in no small measure to a vintage display by Barry John. They were getting very tired by this stage and were anxious to return home, but at the same time they didn't want to squander a 2–1 lead. They were determined to prove that they were the best. Their mood had changed during the tour. When they arrived, they probably believed deep down that the All Blacks were invincible. By the finish, it was they who thought they were almost invincible.

Before the match, the Lions captain, the Welsh back John Dawes, simply said to the players, 'We have come this far. We're not going to throw it away now.' Dawes looked each player in the eye. Further words were superfluous. Each player knew what he had to do.

Spurred on like a wounded animal by the ire of a fanatical nation, the All Blacks started like a whirlwind, taking the lead after just four minutes courtesy of a soft try from Wayne Cottrell. The tension got to the Lions and they underperformed. However, when they were trailing 14–11, J.P.R. Williams dropped a goal from about 40 yards to tie the match.

On the non-playing side, Lynch's greatest memory of the Lions tour is of visiting a vineyard. He had red wine, white wine, blue wine and everything that was going. Smiling like a nun with concussion, he claimed that rugby was the curse of the drinking class!

## Tony the teenage prodigy

Rugby players sometimes suffer from 'Orson Welles syndrome'. Like the famous star of the screen, their crowning moment of glory came at the very start of their careers. Nothing that followed could match it.

Tony O'Reilly became a rugby superstar on the Lions tour to South Africa in 1955, even though he was still a teenage novice at international rugby. Having first been capped against France as an 18 year old in 1955, he really made his mark with the Lions. O'Reilly's quick wit was evident on the tour. Asked as to what he had been doing looking the other way as Springbok goal-kicking ace van der Schyff took the kick which could have given South Africa victory over the Lions in the First Test of the 1955 series, he replied, 'I was in direct communion with the Vatican.' Van der Schyff missed and the tourists won 23–22.

## And as for fortune and as for fame

Tours are rugby's tales of the unexpected. One episode which proves the veracity of that remark came in 1951 when Ireland toured South America. It was a total success off the field and a disaster on it. They were the first international team to be beaten by Argentina. When the Irish team got there, they were told they couldn't play any rugby because Eva Peron had just died. They sent the boys in green down to Santiago, Chile, to teach the cadets how to play. After eight days, the cadets beat the Irish.

The team didn't take the playing side very seriously. At one stage Paddy Lawler went missing for a few days and nobody had a clue where he was. When he returned, a team meeting was hastily called. The team manager solemnly announced that he had been talking to Dublin, which was a big deal in 1951, and then looked around menacingly and said, 'I'm deciding whether or not to send some players home.'

Paddy stood up straight away and replied, 'We've been talking among ourselves and we're deciding whether or not we should send you home.'

## Good manners

On a European tour the Australians were informed that the police had received a complaint saying that one of their players retaliated after being spat at by an English supporter. When the management asked the police spokeswoman what the player should do in those circumstances in the future, they were told: 'If someone spits at him, he'll just have to swallow it.'

## From Russia with love

A Russian team touring England asked in broken English for protection at the pharmacy in Heathrow Airport. Security officials were called and they were taken away for interrogation. It was some time before it dawned on the interrogators that the Russians had, in fact, been looking for condoms.

## Up the Pole

A South African university team were on a tour of Poland. Fred the full-back was in the back seat of a hired car in Warsaw one evening, enjoying a few moments of bliss with his new girlfriend, when a policeman came up and shone his torch through the window.

'Do you know you're up a cul-de-sac?' said the copper.

'Oh, sorry, officer,' said Fred. 'I just assumed that she was a Roman Catholic.'

## Kiss me quick

An Australian club team were on tour in England. Unusually, each of the players brought their wives or girlfriends or both. The hooker's wife asked him to kiss her somewhere dirty. He drove her to Soho.

## Feeling sheepish

A club team from Kent went on tour to the Scottish Highlands. They were staying in a very quiet town and asked the hotel barman if it was possible for them to get some women for the night. 'Nothing like that here,' said the barman. 'You want to go out and find yourself a nice sheep.' The guests did so. The problem was that they ended up spending the night in jail. Returning to the hotel the next day, they said to the barman, 'Fine advice that was, telling us to get a nice sheep.'

'Well,' said the barman, 'you didn't have to pick the police sergeant's own sheep!'

## Doctor's orders

A South African team was on tour in New Zealand. The fly-half was a Tom Cruise lookalike and was a big hit with all the ladies at the many parties they attended. One night he struck up a relationship with a Nicole Kidman lookalike and she brought him home and took him to bed. They were in the throes of passion when the woman's husband walked in. 'What the hell do you think you're doing?' he screamed.

'I'm . . . er . . . I'm a doctor and I'm . . . taking your wife's temperature,' stammered the would-be medic.

'Right!' said the husband. 'I hope for your sake that thing's got numbers on it when you take it out!'

# APPENDIX

# Mick Doyle: An Appreciation

As this book was being written in 2004, the news broke that Mick Doyle had been tragically killed in a car accident. It is difficult to comprehend that this man who gave new meaning to the phrase 'larger than life' is no longer with us.

Despite his great achievements as a player, he will be best remembered as coach of the Irish team that captured the Triple Crown in 1985 in such style, and for the 'give it a lash' philosophy he espoused. Yet the carefree exterior masked a warm and generous nature and a great intelligence. He had a mind as sharp as an executioner's axe.

As is obvious from the chapter on Irish players in this book, Mick was the archetypal rugby mischief-maker, miscreant and mad-hatter. Doyler had a wicked sense of humour. He was taking the Irish team for a Sunday morning session in 1986 and his prop forward Jim McCoy was not moving as swiftly as Doyler would have liked. Big Jim was an RUC officer and was brought up in the Protestant tradition. Doyler shouted at him, 'Hurry up, McCoy, or you'll be late for Mass!'

Mick could also laugh at himself. As his waistline expanded vastly after he stopped playing, when he went into a clothes shop he went first to the women's section. It was not because he had developed a penchant for cross-dressing but because he wanted to visit the maternity section to check out if there was something in his size! He also joked that if you want to spend your money and have something to show for it, try eating rich food.

No doubt he is already organising a rugby match among the angels. The rugby world will be a quieter, greyer and poorer place without him.

To paraphrase John Clare:

> May he rest where mortal man has never trod,
> A place where woman never wept,
> there to abide with his Creator, God,
> and sleep as he in childhood sweetly slept.